The
Actor's
Handbook

Ellen Taft, Editor

Capitol Hill Press, Inc.
P.O. Box 12222
Seattle, WA 98102-0222

© **1997 Ellen Taft**
Published by Capitol Hill Press, Inc.
Seattle, WA 98102-0222

Library of Congress Cataloging-in-Publication
1990,1991,1992,1993,1994,1997
Taft, Ellen M., 1951

The Actor's Handbook: Seattle, Portland & The Pacific
Northwest
     1. Performing Arts-Washington Seattle-Directories
     2. Acting-Study and teaching-Washington State-
     Seattle Handbooks, manuals, etc. 3. Performing
     arts-Northwest. Pacific-Directories. 4. Acting-
     Study and teaching-Pacific Northwest-Handbooks,
     manuals, etc.

PN227.S45J371996 790.2'025'797 94-15390
IBSN 09631102-4-1

Printed in the United States of America

formerly written by Jaroslaw, Mark Niche Press

About The Actor's Handbook

This year's Actor's Handbook does not contain The Producer's Guide, nor many of the other sections from previous books. Show biz opportunities in the Northwest have increased greatly, as a result we had to set priorities and cut sections in the book. We chose to continue listing all opportunities, paid or otherwise, for actors to work, to list teachers on a space available basis, but to cut the Producer's Guide chapter, and other sections only tangentially relevant to getting work. Hopefully, the deleted information will be available through LOFT on computer and will be updated more frequently.

Again I would like to thank the originator of *The Actor's Handbook*, Mark Jaroslaw, Dave Silverman, Seattle Equity Liason Officer, and Nurmi Husa of Portland for valued assistance. The staff, Mary Machala, Kathleen Mary, Kurt Younes and Loel Harvey I congratulate for their ability to work in chaos. Special mention should be made to my computer consultant, Arthur Champernowne.

To Be Listed in the Actor's Handbook

Send your listing to:

> Capitol Hill Press, Inc.
> P.O. Box 12222
> Seattle, WA 98102-0222
> Fax: (206) 323-4101

Please include factual information: names, addresses, telephone numbers etc. Please indicate, on the envelope, the section in which you wish to be listed. Teachers, studio or other actor related services should write and ask for an application and details about the application process. The deadline for the 1998 book is September 1, 1997.

To Order The Actor's Handbook

By Mail   Send $19.95 plus 2.25 shipping and handling, Washington Residents add $1.63 sales tax to the above address.

Credit Card   Call (206) 322-Play

TABLE OF CONTENTS

1

The Stage Actor

AUDITION CALENDAR, HOTLINES, & CALLBOARDS

Calendar

- **SEPTEMBER:**
  Taproot Theatre Company
  Portland Center Stage

- **OCTOBER:**
  Civic Light Opera

- **OCTOBER/NOVEMBER:**
  Aha! Theatre
  Eddie May Mysteries

- **NOVEMBER:**
  New City Playwrights' Festival
  New City Second Company

- **NOVEMBER/DECEMBER:**
  Missoula Children's Tours-Issues and Answers

- **DECEMBER/JANUARY:**
  Bathhouse Theatre
  Idaho Shakespeare Festival
  Intiman Theatre
  Missoula Children's Touring Project
  Montana Shakespeare in the Parks
  Northwest Savoyards
  Rainier Stage Company

- **JANUARY/FEBRUARY:**
  Columbia Theatre for the Performing Arts
  Idaho Shakespeare Festival
  Portland Rep Playwrights' Festival

- **FEBRUARY:**
  Idaho Repertory Theatre Company
  Northwest Drama Conference Auditions
  Seattle Gilbert & Sullivan Society

1.1 Calendar

■ **FEBRUARY/MARCH:**
    Coeur d'Alene Summer Theatre
    Greenstage

■ **MARCH**
    Fishnet Theatre
    Laughing Horse Summer Theatre
    Perseverance Theater
    Tacoma Actors Guild
    Tears of Joy
    Virginia City Players

■ **MARCH/APRIL:**
    Seattle Children's Theatre

■ **APRIL:**
    The Group Theatre
    Seattle Repertory Theatre

■ **APRIL/MAY:**
    Camlann Medieval Faire
    Seattle Shakespeare Festival
    Snoqualmie Falls Forest Theatre

■ **MAY:**
    Brown Bag Theatre/
        Willie The Shake's Summer Shorts
    Civic Light Opera
    Tacoma Actors Guild
    University of Portland/Muck's Crest Productions
    Wooden "O" Theater Productions

■ **MAY/JUNE**
    Highliners Performing Organization
    Portland Repertory Theatre
    Seattle Repertory Theatre

■ **JUNE:**
    The Group Theatre
    Fifth Avenue Musical Theatre
    The Village Theatre

1.1 Calendar

- **JUNE/JULY:**
  Center Stage

- **JULY:**
  Center Stage
  The Empty Space Theatre
  Miranda Theater/Milagro Theatre
  New City — Actors/Director's Festival
  Northwest Savoyards
  Rainier Stage Company

- **AUGUST:**
  Emerald City Players
  Fishnet Theatre
  The Group Cultural Enrichment Program
  New City — Actor's/Directors Festival
  Spokane Interplayers Ensemble
  Sprouts Children's Theatre

Seattle Hotlines

- **Equity**   **(206) 637-7332**
- **LOFT (non-Equity)**   **(206) 637-7373**
- **Seattle Times**   **(206) 464-2000**
                                     ext. 2787
- **Film Information**   **(206) 464-6074**

Portland Hotline

- **PATA**   **(503) 241-4902**
- **U/Talent**
18 West Mercer St. #200
Seattle, WA 98119
1-800-404-5966 (USPAN, Inc.)

Union exclusive service showcasing headshots/resumes on the Internet. One year exposure for $100, or call for pricing (206) 281-1112.

1.1 Calendar

National Equity Hotlines

- Atlanta, GA (404) 257-2575
- Boston, MA (617) 720-6048
- Buffalo, NY (716)883-1767
- Chicago, IL (312) 641-0418
- Cleveland, OH (216) 779-2001
- Dallas/Ft. Worth, TX (214) 922-7843
- Denver (303) 757-1216
- Detroit, MI (810) 552-0520
- Florida-Central (407) 345-9322
- Florida-South (954) 421-2777
- Houston, TX (713) 917-4564
- Kansas City, MO (816) 531-4841
- Los Angeles, CA (213) 462-0955
- Milwaukee/Madison (414) 963-4023
- Minneapolis/St. Paul (612) 371-0689
- New York City, NY (212) 869-1242
- Philadelphia, PA (215) 785-2232
- Phoenix (602) 265-7117
- Pittsburgh (412) 741-3360
- San Diego, CA (619) 595-3890
- San Francisco, CA (415) 434-8007
- St. Louis, MO (314) 851-0906
- Washington D.C./Baltimore (202) 722- 7350

Public Callboards

- **THE PLAY'S THE THING**

514 E Pike
Seattle, WA 98122
(206) 322-PLAY

> Seattle's drama bookstore has an audition board.

Newspaper Callboards

Seattle

■ **SEATTLE POST-INTELLIGENCER**
Auditions section in What's Happening, every Friday.

■ **THE STRANGER**
Theatre Listing section, every Wednesday or Thursday.

Tacoma

■ **NEWS TRIBUNE**
Prints notices in Friday's TGIF section.

Portland

■ **THE OREGONIAN**
Prints notices in Friday's paper.

■ **WILLAMETTE WEEK**
Audition notices on Wednesday.

EQUITY THEATRE

The Northwest

■ **A CONTEMPORARY THEATRE** (LORT C)
700 Union St.
Seattle, WA 98101
(206) 292-7660
Fax: (206) 292-7670

Artistic Director: Peggy Shannon. Founded in 1965, ACT recently moved from Queen Anne to its new multi-stage theatre located in the historic Eagles Auditorium Building, in downtown Seattle adjacent to the Washington State Convention Center. ACT presents six mainstage productions, including new and contemporary works, between May and November, as well as *A Christmas Carol* in December. The Young ACT Company tours Northwest public schools, grades K through 6, in January and February, using six to eight multicultural actors. ACT welcomes multicultural actors to apply for all parts and plays.

Season auditions are held between October and February, and are announced on the Equity Hotline; appointments are made by mail. Auditions for Young Act Company are held at the end of November or the beginning of December. Internships are offered in production and office administration only. Contact: for actors, Casting Director, Margaret Layne; for directors, Peggy Shannon; for stage managers, designers and technicians, General Manager, Jim Verdery.

■ **THE BATHHOUSE THEATRE** (SPT)
7312 West Greenlake Dr. N
Seattle, WA 98103
(206) 783-0053
Fax: (206) 784-3966

Artistic Director: Arne Zaslove. Seattle's original theatre ensemble commemorates its 27th anniversary in 1997. Between February and December, The Bathhouse has scheduled five productions: a combination of classics, musical revues, and new works on popular culture.

The company holds open auditions in the second week of January; preference is given to actors with singing and classical text skills. The theatre operates on an SPT contract. Contact: for actors, Production Manager, Dale Melsmess; for stage managers, directors and designers, Managing Director, Arne Zaslove. Web site: http://www.seattlesquare.com/bathhouse

■ **CENTER STAGE** (SPT)
3801 E Mercer Way
Mercer Island, WA 98040
(206) 232-7115
Fax: (206) 232-7119

Cultural Arts Director: Steve Alter. The Northwest's first professional Jewish theatre is dedicated to producing contemporary plays that reflect universal concerns from a uniquely Jewish perspective. The company produces three shows at the Stroum Jewish Center between November and March, and tours a Holocaust show January through May.

General auditions are held in the summer, with callbacks on a show-by-show basis. Auditions are announced on the Equity Hotline and in the newspapers, and appointments are made by mail; send resume anytime. Center Stage casts both Jewish and non-Jewish actors. The theatre operates on a SPT contract (AEA/Category 1-2); Equity pay is currently $125-150 per week;

1.2 Equity

non-Equity pay is $50-100 per week. Contact: for actors, stage managers, directors, designers and technicians, Steve Alter.

■ **THE EMPTY SPACE THEATRE** (LOA)
3509 Fremont Ave. N
Seattle, WA 98103
(206) 547-7633
Fax: (206) 547-7635

Artistic Director: Eddie Levi Lee. Founded in 1970, the Empty Space is one of the country's leading regional theatres; its classics are offbeat, and its contemporary works are usually new, risky and theatrically exciting. Of 157 mainstage shows, 80% have been regional or world premieres. Six works are planned between September and July.

A general audition is held mid-summer. The theatre also periodically holds mini-general auditions for actors new to Seattle. Contact: for actors and directors, Eddie Levi Lee or Production Manager, Becky Barnett; for designers and technicians, Technical Director, Rod Pilloud. Web site: http://emptyspace.com

■ **FIFTH AVENUE MUSICAL THEATRE** (WCLO)
1308 Fifth Ave.
Seattle, WA 98101
(206) 625-1418
Fax: (206) 292-9610

Executive Director: Frank Young. Seattle's historic downtown theatre, once known for its touring Broadway musicals, is now producing locally, in affiliation with Houston's Theatre Under the Stars. They produce four musicals between October and April. Some productions also tour.

Regional auditions are held each summer for Equity and non-Equity talent. Audition appointments are made by phone several weeks before the auditions. Note: some straight dramatic roles (for character parts) will be available, but bring sheet music and be prepared to sing; you might be requested to do so. Contact for actors, stage managers and directors, Frank Young; theatre does not hire designers. Web site: http://speakeasy.org/5thavenue

■ **THE GROUP THEATRE** (SPT)
305 Harrison St.
Seattle, WA 98109
(206) 441-9480
Fax: (206) 441-9838

Artistic Director: José Carrasquillo. The Group Theatre's multi-ethnic company explores cultural, political and minority themes, with emphasis on playwrights of color. Three productions, drama, comedy and revue, are scheduled between September and June at the Carlton Playhouse in the lower level of (Seattle) Center House. The Group also offers a Cultural Enrichment Program that tours the public schools in the fall/spring.

Auditions are held for the mainstage between April and June, and for the tour in August. The Group operates on an SPT-Category 7 contract, currently $285/week minimum for mainstage productions; non-Equity pay is $270/week minimum. Readings for plays-in-development vary. Internships are available. Contact: for directors, José Carrasquillo; for stage managers, designers and technicians, Technical Director, Rex Carleton.

■ **INTIMAN THEATRE** (LORT C)
P.O. Box 19760
Seattle, WA 98109-1760
(206) 269-1901 ext. 351
Fax (206) 269-1928

Artistic Director: Warner Shook. Seattle's most popular theatre ensemble schedules six productions between May and December at its Seattle Center theatre. Intiman also has the Living History/Arts in Schools

1.2 Equity

Program, a multicultural residency program. Eight
actors/teachers of diverse cultural backgrounds perform
plays/workshops in public schools, grades K-6, touring
throughout western and central Washington. Actors of
color are encouraged to apply for all parts and plays.

Annual auditions are held for the mainstage in
January, by appointment only, and for the touring in the
fall. Mainstage contact: for actors, Assistant Art Director,
Janine Zeller; for stage managers, directors and designers,
Production Manager, David Milligan. Touring program
contact: Education Director, Colby Wilk; send resume,
photo and letter of interest; Equity and non-Equity
performers are hired for program. Web site: http://
www.seattlesquare.com/intiman

■ **NEW CITY THEATER & ARTS CENTER**
   THEATER ZERO (SPT)
   1634 11th Ave.
   Seattle, WA 98122
   (206) 323-6801

Artistic Director: John Kazanjian. New City sponsors
a Playwrights'/Actors' Festival in the fall, film festival,
late-night cabaret and dance performances, as well as two
acting companies, Theater Zero and Second Company.
Theater Zero is an Equity company that produces two to
three mainstage shows annually, a mixture of company-
developed work, national collaborations and projects with
playwrights-in-residence. Second Company is a non-
Equity company (see 1.4 Fringe Theatre).

Auditions are held for Theater Zero on a show-by-
show basis, if at all; for the Playwrights' Festival in the
late fall; and for other shows on a show-by-show basis.
Auditions are announced in newspaper callboards.
Contact: for Theater Zero and other productions, Manager
of Theater Zero, Karen Uffelman; for Second Company
productions, Director of Second Company, Rosa Josie.

1.2 Equity

Web site:http://weber.u.washington.edu/~jabourne/theater/newcity.html

■ OREGON SHAKESPEARE FESTIVAL (LORT B)
P.O. Box 158
Ashland, OR 97520
(206) 482-2111
Fax: (541) 482-2111

Artistic Director: Libby Apple. OSF, a 1983 Tony award winner and the nation's largest regional repertory company, kicks off its 62nd year in February 1997. By October, the Festival's more than 70 performers will have produced 11 classic and contemporary productions, in three theatres, with ticket sales in excess of 350,000. OSF also does a School Tour in the fall/spring.

Auditions are conducted January through June, for the following year's season, in Los Angeles, New York City, Chicago and other locations; contact your local Equity office. Write or call for auditions. Internships are offered in all areas of theatre. Contact: for actors and others, Personnel Assistant, Patricia Leonard. Web site: http://www.mind.net/osf

■ PORTLAND CENTER STAGE
P.O. Box 9008
Portland, OR 97207
(503) 248-6309
Fax: (503) 796-6509

Artistic Director: Elizabeth Huddle. PCS produces five shows in season running from October to May; theatre is located at 1111 SW Broadway in Portland.

General auditions are held in September; they are announced in local papers. PCS pays Equity rates. Some internships are available. Contact: for actors and others, Company Manager, Rose Riordan.

1.2 Equity

■ **PORTLAND REPERTORY THEATRE** (SPT)
815 NW 12th
Portland, OR 97204
(503) 224-9221
Fax: (503) 224-1316

Artistic Director/Producer: Dennis Bigelow. The oldest of Portland's Equity houses has five productions scheduled between October and May, offering a blend of Broadway, off-Broadway, and American classics. Additional plays are produced as part of PRT's Young Playwright Festival.

General auditions are held in late May to early June for the following season's shows; they are announced in Portland papers and Portland/Seattle Equity hotlines. Equity pay is $325/week minimum plus housing; non-Equity varies. Actors contact: Dennis Bigelow.

■ **SEATTLE CHILDREN'S THEATRE** (TYA)
P.O. Box 9640
Seattle, WA 98109-0640
(206) 443-0807
Fax: (206) 443-0442

Artistic Director: Linda Hartzell. The nation's second largest resident children's theatre company produces six mainstage shows, including musicals, classics, comedies, fairy tales and contemporary social works, and performs one play at schools throughout the school year. The company is in its 22nd season, and fourth year at the Charlotte Martin Theatre, a 485-seat state-of-the-art facility at the Seattle Center. SCT schedules weekday performances for grades K through 12, and weekend performaces for family audiences, with 11 shows a week in all, plus post-play discussions.

Season auditions are held in spring, with callbacks throughout the year. Audtions are announced in local papers and the Equity Hotline. The Production Stage Manager, Linda Jo Brooke, maintains an active file for actors and stage managers; send photo and resume. SCT does not currently offer internships, but may do so in the future. Contact: for directors, Linda Hartzell; for designers, Technical Director, Silas Morse.

■ **SEATTLE REPERTORY THEATRE**
(LORT B/LORT D)
155 Mercer St.
Seattle, WA 98109
(206) 443-2210
Fax: (206) 443-2379

Artistic Director: Sharon Ott. Associate Artistic Director: David Saint. The Rep, the oldest Equity theatre in Seattle, is one of the nation's top regional theatres. The Rep produces both a mainstage and Stage II season between October and May, plus a spring series of workshop productions of new plays in progress. Five shows, including two world premiers in 1997, are presented on the mainstage. Three shows, including two world premiers in 1997, are presented on the second stage; the new Stage II Theatre opens in January 1997.

The Rep's educational touring unit, known as the Mobile Outreach Bunch (MOB), is celebrating its 20th year, and will tour in the spring under the auspices of the Cultural Enrichment Program. This is a TYA contract for four to five actors in a commissioned new work.

Season auditions are conducted in Seattle in the spring/summer. Supplemental auditions are held as needed throughout the season, and visiting Equity members are invited to make an audition appointment. Internships are available. Contact: for actors and directors, Artistic Administrator, Peggy Scales; for designers and stage managers, Production Manager, Juli Ann Clifton; for MOB, TedSod.
Web site: http://www.seattlesquare.com/therep

1.2 Equity

■ **SEATTLE SHAKESPEARE FESTIVAL** (SPT/TYA)

(See 1.11 Shakespeare.)

■ **TACOMA ACTORS GUILD** (LOA)
Jones Building, 6th Floor
901 Broadway Plaza
Tacoma, WA 98102   98402
(206) 272-3107
Fax: (206) 272-3358

Producing Artistic Director: Pat Patton. TAG, currently in its 18th season, has six scheduled productions between October and April, including contemporary and new works, and an American musical. The theatre is located at 915 Broadway Plaza.

TAG typically conducts an annual call between March and May, and then holds callbacks show-by-show. Actors are urged to audition during the generals. Visiting Equity members and those new to the area may send a photo/resume to request a mid-year audition; TAG will accommodate them if possible. Contact: for actors, Associate Artistic Director, Kamella Tate; for stage managers, directors and designers, Pat Patton.

NON-UNION PROFESSIONAL THEATRE

Washington

■ **BROWN BAG THEATRE**
2000 Second Ave. Suite 308
Seattle, WA 98121
(206) 443-2530

Contact: Kathleen Mary, Director. Brown Bag features a season of downtown lunchtime one-acts during fall, winter and spring. In July and August, shortened Shakespeare shows, *Willie the Shake's Summer Shorts*, are performed outside at different downtown locations, usually at plazas, parks and on the streets. In addition to the lunch time offerings, Brown Bag also presents evening full-length plays. Actors are paid $50-$100 a week. Casting is done through LOFT generals and periodically; please check callboards and the non-Equity (LOFT) Hotline.

■ **CIVIC LIGHT OPERA**
P.O. Box 75672
Northgate Station
Seattle, WA 98125
(206) 363-4807

Contact Jeff Vaughn, Production Manager. Now in its 20th season, CLO produces four musicals between September and May in an 1,100 seat auditorium. CLO has a large subscriber base, generally filling at least two-thirds of the house. All roles are paid, with variations between leads and ensemble. They specialize in the standard, classic musical theater repertoire, including Rogers and Hammerstein, and Gilbert and Sullivan.

1.3 Professional Theatre

Dancing is required for one of the productions. CLO holds generals in May and October. Check local press and callboards for auditions.

■ **EDGE OF THE WORLD THEATRE**
9792 Edmonds Way
Box 260
Edmonds, WA 98020
(206) 542-PLAY

Contact: Michael Kelley, Artistic Director. A non-Equity professional theatre producing seven productions in a 47-week season. Productions include musicals, comedies, dramas, and other mainstream theatre. All performing and technical positions are paid. The theatre is always accepting resumes. Check local newspaper callboards.

■ **G.A.P. THEATRE**
115 Blanchard St.
Seattle, WA 98121-2020
(206) 448-7575
(206) 448-7585

Contact: G. Valmont Thomas, Managing Assistant Director. Growth and Prevention Company (G.A.P.) is a professional musical theatre that produces original works created by Northwest theatre artists. Productions focus on topics such as self-esteem, substance abuse, diversity, the environment and racism. The resident company performs six shows, September through June, at schools, community centers and for government and corporate training sessions throughout the Northwest. Actors are paid $100/week for rehearsals, $65/performance with four performances per week, Monday through Friday, 8 a.m. to 5 p.m. Actors and singers of all ethnic backgrounds are encouraged to send photos/resumes year-round. General season auditions are held March and August. The company calls people who are on file and announces auditions on hotlines and in local newspaper callboards.

■ **NOTHING SACRED PRODUCTIONS**
14623 N E 43rd Place
Bellevue, WA 98007
(206) 867-9756

Contact: Stan Gill, Artistic Director. Nothing Sacred produces three to four plays a year September through June. Auditions are show-by-show. Actors receive a stipend, directors are paid a fee. Check local press and LOFT Hotline for audition notices. E-mail: stageguy1@aol.com

■ **RENTON CIVIC THEATRE**
P.O. Box 1556
Renton, WA 98057
(206) 226-5529

Contact: Rick May, Artistic Director. Founded eight years ago, Renton Civic is a semi-professional theatre which produces six shows, three musicals, one comedy and one classic per year in a 322-seat auditorium, plus one summer production.   Actors are paid $150 per show. Auditions are announced in newspaper callboards on a show-by-show basis.

■ **SPOKANE INTERPLAYERS ENSEMBLE**
P.O. Box 1961
Spokane, WA 99210
(509) 455-7529

In its 16th season, eastern Washington's ranking theatre company usually schedules seven productions (comedy, classics, contemporary and new works) between September and June. Artistic directors, Joan and Bob Welch, conduct season auditions in Seattle in late summer and typically hire about three dozen local actors. Interplayers conducts daily and weekend rehearsals; actors are paid $220 to $260 per week for rehearsals and performances. Efforts are made to help the cast find housing.   E-mail: interplayers@interplayers.com Web: http://www.interplayers.com

1.3 Professional Theatre

■ **SPROUTS CHILDREN'S THEATRE**
14623 NE 43rd Pl.
Bellevue, WA 98007
(206) 827-3123

Contact: Stan Gill. This children's theatre, devoted to presenting original musical productions on the Eastside, produces one to five shows per year. General audition is in late summer; auditions are also held on a show-by-show as-needed basis. Actors are paid $20 to $30 per performance. Check local press and LOFT Hotline for audition notices. Performances are at Studio East.

■ **TAPROOT THEATRE COMPANY**
204 N 85th St.
Seattle, WA 98103
(206) 781-9705

Contact Pam Nolte. TTC's five-play season runs February through October. Founded in 1976, TTC is dedicated to producing works "that reflect a belief in the dignity of people, and the virtue of faith as exemplified in the Judeo/Christian tradition." Season auditions are held in the early fall. All positions are paid, varying from stipends to Arts Paymaster, depending upon the program (the improv 'team', the touring company, the mainstage production, or the Christmas dinner theater). Check local newspaper callboards and the LOFT Hotline for audition notices.

1.3 Professional Theatre

■ **TEARS OF JOY**
1109 E Fifth St.
Vancouver, WA 98661
(360) 695-3050
Fax: (360) 695-0438

Contact: Reg Bradley, Artistic Director. Tear of Joy produces three touring shows and five mainstage shows per year, September to May. Directors and actors are paid. Send resume anytime; check local newspaper callboards and the PATA Hotline for audition notices.

■ **THE VILLAGE THEATRE**
303 Front Street N
Issaquah, WA 98027
(206) 392-1942
Fax: (206) 391-3242

Contact: Ken Tilden, Production Manager. The Village Theatre is the Eastside's primary producing theatre, having recently acquired a second building which houses their rehearsal space and 488-seat mainstage. The old space is currently utilized in the creation and performance of new musicals which premiere in the First Stage series each summer. Each season TVT presents three major musicals, one comedy and one drama, all family-oriented. TVT pays $28 per rehearsal and per performance. Auditions held annually. Check local press callboards and LOFT Hotline. Web site: www.vt.org

1.3 Professional Theatre

Alaska

■ **PERSERVERANCE THEATRE**
914 Third Street
Douglas, AK 99824
(907)364-2421 ext. 8
Fax: (907) 364-2603

    Contact: Molly Smith, Artistic Director. PT produces a full season of classic and contemporary plays, as well as a play-reading festival. Internships are available. Auditions are held in the spring; preference is given to Alaska residents. Contact Molly Smith to schedule an audition. Actors are paid $1,850 a month; interns are paid $1,100 a month. E-mail: persthr@ptialaska.net Web site: www.juneau.com/pt/

Oregon

■ **KAISER PERMANENTE**
500 NE Multnomah #100
Portland, OR 97214
(503) 813-4859
Fax: (503) 813-4576

    Contact: Rene King, Production Manager. Kaiser Permanente presents educational theatre to schools free of charge, with a focus on children's health and safety. It tours two plays a year in northwest Oregon and southwest Washington, fall to spring. It offers six-month contracts at non-union wages. Auditions are held in fall and spring. Check Oregon press for notices.

1.3 Professional Theatre

■ **MIRANDA THEATER/THEATRE MILAGRO**
425 SE Sixth
Portland, OR 97214
(503) 236-7253
Fax (503) 236-4174

Contact: Jose Gonzales. The theatre presents Hispanic arts and cultural programs, producing six shows, September to June. Actors are paid on a sliding scale. Check Portland press and PATA Hotline for audition notices. E-mail: www.milagro.org

■ **MUSICAL THEATRE COMPANY**
1436 SW Montgomery
Portland, OR 97201
(503) 240-1859

Contact: Jutta Allen, Managing Director. Musical Theatre Company produces five plays a year, October to July. Actors are paid a stipend. Auditions are held on a show-by-show basis; check Portland press and PATA Hotline.

■ **NORTHWEST CHILDREN'S THEATRE**
1819 NW Everett St. #206
Portland, OR 97209
(503) 222-2190
Fax: (503)222-4130

Contact: John Monteverde, Artistic Director. Produces eight family-oriented shows from September through June. Actors are paid $300 to $500 for a three-week contract. NCT hires actors of all ages. Check Portland press, PATA Hotline and *Oregonian* callboard for audition notices.

1.3 Professional Theatre

■ OREGON STAGE COMPANY
5340 N Interstate Ave.
Portland, OR 97217
(503) 287-5929

Contact: Laurel Nagoda. Oregon Stage Company
performs in the 215-seat Forum Theatre on the Rock Creek
campus of Portland Community College. Their season
runs October through May, including a holiday show in
December. They produce an eclectic mix of occasional
new works, classics, and usually one small musical. Non-
union actors receive a per-performance stipend; Equity
actors are paid through an umbrella contract: $100/week
for rehearsals, $125/week for performances. Auditions
are held on an as-needed basis in Portland; they also attend
the semi-annual PATA auditions.

■ TAPESTRY THEATRE
P. O. Box 19844
Portland, OR 97280
(503) 245-6919
Fax: (503) 244-5421

Contact: Judy Straalsund, Artistic Director. Tapestry
presents three to four shows from fall to spring, in order
to "challenge people of all beliefs, yet ultimately glorify
God." The season includes both original work and classics
such as *Enemy of the People* and *The Four Poster*. They also
produce a serial Christmas show which annually updates
the story of a Renaissance-era family, in addition to
sponsoring a school-tour show in the spring. Tapestry
pays an average of $10 per performance: $25 for lead
actors, $5-$10 for smaller roles. Auditions are held two to
three times a year; check Portland papers for notices.
E-mail: http://www.teleport.com/nonprofit/tapestry

1.3 Professional Theatre

<u>Montana</u>

■ **MISSOULA CHILDREN'S THEATRE**
200 N Adams
Missoula, MT 59802
(406) 728-1911
Fax: (406) 721-0637

Contact: Don Kukla. MCT, in its 25th year, is dedicated to the enhancement of the life skills of children via participation in the performing arts. The company presents original musical adaptations of classic fairy tales. Touring year-round, the company presents 21 productions from 13 titles. MCT has two separate touring companies: the MCT Touring Project, which tours year-round through the U.S., Canada and Pacific Rim countries, and the Issues and Answers School Tour, which tours January through April, primarily in the Northwest. The actors are paid $18, 000 per year, with benefits for actors with seniority. MCT holds auditions at major regional drama/theatre conferences. Call for information, or check their web site; mail photo/resume and/or video January through March for the first tour, November through December for their second tour. E-mail: tour@mctinc.org Web site: httrp://www.mctinc.org

FRINGE THEATRE

Washington

■ **ALICE B. ARTS**
1100 E. Pike St. #1111
Seattle, WA 98122
(206) 322-5423 (32-ALICE)

Artistic Director: Drew Emery. Alice B. is a provocative, irreverent and controversial producer of largely interdisciplinary works with a high focus on creating collaborative new work. Alice B. Arts (formerly Alice B. Theatre) is dedicated to building community through gay- and lesbian-centered artistic and cultural events for all. It generally pays for performances, plus a stipend for rehearsal; Equity umbrella agreements under Arts Paymaster. Alice B. holds auditions announced year-round. Unsolicited resumes/headshots are not recommended; volunteer and community involvement is encouraged.

■ **ACME THEATRICKS**
1622 N Ninth St.
Tacoma, WA. 98403
(206) 627-7301

Contact: Madge Montgomery. Acme explores community issues in new works by Northwest playwrights; it performs three to four plays a year. Acme attracts younger, risk-taking actors. It pays a small stipend, usually around $50. Acme announces auditions in newspaper callboards and on LOFT Hotline, and attends LOFT generals.

■ **AHA! THEATRE**
P.O. Box 19880
Seattle, WA 98109
2222 Second Ave. 98121
(206) 728-8059

Contact: Allison M. Halstead or Jeffrey Paul Reid. AHA! produces an eclectic season featuring contemporary drama, new works, and alternative interpretations of the classics. AHA!'s season runs from January through the fall of each year. It was voted "Best Fringe" by *Seattle Weekly* readers in 1995 & 96. AHA! has two stages (85-seat and 50-seat) as well as a small cabaret space that seats 35. Full-season auditions are held each fall. Consult local press callboards. The theatre does some shows with Arts Pay Master equity contract.

■ **ANNEX THEATRE**
1916 Fourth Ave.
Seattle, WA 98101
(206) 728-8081
Fax: (206) 728-1735

Contact: Andrea Allen. Annex is home to theatre artists who commit to developing new works that challenge traditional expectations of the theatrical experience. It produces nine shows a year, plus a Christmas show. Actors are paid a small stipend. Check the Annex audition hotline for current notices.

■ **BELLTOWN THEATRE CENTER**
115 Blanchard
Seattle, WA 98121
(206) 728-7609

Contact: Larry Silverberg, Artistic Director. "BTC's mission is to explore the human condition through the production of great modern dramatic literature so we may awaken the hearts and touch the lives of all who come into our home." BTC produces four shows a season, as

1.4 Fringe

well as the "Belltown Reads" new play series each September. Larry Silverberg heads BTC's Meisner technique training program. For audition information, check local press callboards or LOFT Hotline.

■ **BELLEVUE OPERA/PECCADILLO PLAYERS**
8726 NE 11th
Bellevue, WA 98004
(206) 454-1906

    Contact: Penelope Vrachopoulos. Now in its 24th year, Bellevue Opera specializes in Gilbert and Sullivan and pre-1914 operettas and light opera. Auditions are show-to-show; check newspaper callboards.

■ **BRICOLAGE**
1624 - 31st Ave.
Seattle, WA 98122
(206) 324-8053

    Contact: Gretchen Johnston. Bricolage concentrates on un-produced and under-produced works. Four shows per year; consult the LOFT Hotline and newspaper callboards. Attends LOFT generals.

■ **GREEK ACTIVE**
1120 17th Ave. #203
Seattle, WA. 98122
(206) 516-1125

    Contact: David Morden. Greek Active produces approximately three shows per year, doing "queer re-contextualizations of the classics," performing in bars because "we like to." It does no AIDS dramas because "we're *living* AIDS dramas." Greek Active takes to heart the saying: "Dying is easy, comedy is hard." The company hires gay or straight actors, and splits the box office receipts. Check local press callboards for audition information.

■ GUERILLA MEDIA PRODUCTIONS
c/o Craig Thompson
1100 - 17th Ave. #406
Seattle, WA. 98122
(206) 323-8502

Contact: Craig Thompson. A semi-professional company founded in 1992, GMP specializes in multimedia stage productions, employing slide imagery and recording equipment. GMP is open to working with other companies and individuals on interesting and unusual projects. Scripts are often generated through improvisation in the rehearsal process. Pay depends on the show. A LOFT member theatre; check the LOFT hotline and local callboards for auditions.

■ THE IMMEDIATE THEATRE
1616 Queen Anne Ave. N #206
Seattle, WA. 98109-2859
Tel. and Fax (206) 301-9945

Contact: Chuck Hudson, Artistic Director. Founded in 1994, The Immediate Theatre is committed to the creation of visually exciting dramatic works. Company members master various movement and performance techniques in order to "re-shape the spoken word and make the invisible visible." It produces two ensemble generated/site specific shows per season, one of which is an original creation. Auditions are on a show-by-show basis; check the LOFT Hotline and local callboards for notices. Actors are non-equity and are paid a stipend. E-mail: immediate@aol.com

1.4 Fringe

■ LEAP OF FAITH THEATRE
7734 - 13th Ave. NW
Seattle, WA 98117
(206) 789-2689
Fax: (206) 784-5177

Contact: Cornelia Duryee. Formerly the Deeply Moving Dance Co., this company is a collaboration of dancers, actors and playwrights whose performances often incorporate many disciplines, from ballet to straight drama. Leap of Faith Theatre sponsors a new play contest called the Jumpstart New Play Contest each Spring. Leap of Faith can use equity actors through Arts Paymaster. Auditions are held on a show-by-show basis; Leap of Faith also attends LOFT generals. Consult the callboards and LOFT Hotline.

■ LOCAL ACCESS
118 - 27th Ave. E
Seattle, WA 98112
Tel. and Fax: (206) 329-4883 (To fax, call first)

Contact: Jan Maher. Projects representative of Local Access' mission include "Plays To Go," presenting multicultural theatre in "readers' theatre" format, and New Options, a program that educates young audiences about violence within relationships through interactive peformances. Consult newspaper callboards and LOFT and Equity Hotlines. Local Access attends LOFT generals.

■ LOOKING GLASS THEATRE
1605 First Ave. W
Seattle, WA. 98119
(206) 781-3990

Contact: Mona Al-Haddad, Producing Director. Looking Glass seeks to confront prejudice and discrimination with challenging, evocative and transformative shows. The theatre pays a small stipend. Looking Glass welcomes headshots/resumes, and attends LOFT Generals. Check local press callboards and LOFT Hotline.

■ MUSIC THEATRE WORKS
10430 Lake City Way NE
Seattle, WA. 98125
(206) 524-3717

Contact: Tammis Doyle. Founded in January 1990, Music Theatre Works sponsors workshops and full productions of various musical theatre forms. It needs singing actors to workshop original scripts. MTW attends LOFT Generals; check local callboards. (Formerly The Music Theatre Workshop.)

■ NW ASIAN AMERICAN THEATRE
409 Seventh Ave. S
Seattle, WA 98104
(206) 340-1445

Contact: Kathy Hsieh. In its 24th season, Northwest Asian American Theatre produces five to six shows per year and an annual talent show. Its season runs from October to June. Its new works explore Asian-American issues, providing opportunites for Asian-American actors, directors and designers. Pay is $200 to $300 per run (15 to 22 performances) for non-union actors. Occasionally, Equity actors are hired under Arts Paymaster. Casts are often ethnically mixed. Audition notices are posted on the NWAAT hotline at (206) 340-1049, box 3. The theatre also participates in the LOFT general auditions, and announces auditions in local newspaper callboards.

■ ONE WORLD THEATRE
P.O. Box 85454
Seattle, WA 98145
(206) 632-6553
Fax: (206) 548-0105

Contact: Jena Cane. An international touring ensemble, founded in 1988, One World brings theatrical events to communities throughout the Northwest and Canada. OWT runs the Rainier Performing Arts Project,

1.4 Fringe

an arts education program for youth in southeast Seattle. OWT also collaborates with social and arts groups to produce new works and adaptations of classics. Tours begin in June. All acting positions are paid. One World seeks a multicultural ensemble. Check newspaper callboards.

■ **OPEN CIRCLE THEATRE**
429 Boren Ave. N.
Seattle, WA. 98109
(206) 516-4149

Contact: Christopher Petit, Artistic Director. Open Circle has been in existence for five years, producing colorful versions of new and old texts that "lend themselves to high theatricality." OCT presents four workshop productions and four mainstage shows per year. Auditions are held on a show-by-show basis; OCT also attends LOFT Generals. Check local newspaper callboards for announcements.

■ **PILGRIM CENTER FOR THE ARTS**
509 Tenth Ave. E
Seattle, WA 98102
(206) 323-4034
Fax: (206) 323-3727

Contact: Mark Williams, Managing Artistic Director. Pilgrim Center for the Art is a not-for-profit neighborhood arts center in Capitol Hill's turn-of-the-century Pilgrim Congregational Church. As an independent organization, PCA sponsors resident theatre companies, a summer theatre festival, music and dance productions, poetry readings and gallery displays. Actors are paid a small stipend, or work occasionally through Arts Paymaster. Auditions are held on a show-by-show basis; PCA also attends LOFT Generals. E-mail: pilgrim@pilgrim.org Website: www.pilgrim.org

■ **PRESENT COMPANY THEATRE**
c/o S. P. Miskowski
1202 E. Pike #950
Seattle, WA 98122-3934
(206) 325-1440

   Contact: S. P. Miskowski. Present Company, headed
by the former managing editor of Seattle's alternative
newspaper *The Stranger,* produces two to three shows
per year. Generally, the shows are written by Miskowski,
although one show per season is created collaboratively
by actors, designers and playwright. Pay varies
depending on box-office receipts. Check newspaper
callboards. E-mail: spmisko@aol.com

■ **REALLY BIG PRODUCTION CO.**
2043 13th Ave. W
Seattle, WA 98119
(206) 441-3639

   Contact: Mark Nichols. Produces two original
musicals per year, generally created by Mark Nichols.
RBP also accepts original script/music submissions. RBP
is particularly interested in actors with unusual vocal
talent. A small stipend is paid to actors; the amount
depends on box office receipts. Auditions on a show-by-
show basis; check local press callboards and hotlines.

■ **REPERTORY ACTORS WORKSHOP (ReAct)**
5448 N 50th St.
Ruston, WA 98407
(206) 364-3283

   Contact: David Hsieh. ReAct presents popular
mainstream works, but casts multiculturally and non-
traditionally. It seeks to give artists the opportunity to
work on projects they do not normally have access to due
to race, age, sex or experience. ReAct uses its productions
to raise money for charitable and humanitarian
organizations throughout the Pacific Northwest. It

1.4 Fringe

produces one to four shows per season. ReAct attends LOFT Generals.

■ SEATTLE PUBLIC THEATER
915 E Pine #426
Seattle, WA 98122
(206) 328-4848
Fax: (206)322-5569

    Contact: Marc Weinblatt. SPT has been in existence for nine years, specializing in non-realistic, socially responsible touring plays, as well as the interactive *Theatre of Liberation* program based on Augusto Boals' "theatre of the oppressed." SPT leads workshops and presents performances as a means of empowerment, education and transformation. All positions are paid. Check local press callboards; SPT also attends LOFT Generals. E-mail:marco59@aol.com

■ SEATTLE THEATRE PROJECT
2305 First Ave #314
Seattle, WA 98121
(206) 441-4837

    Contact: Lisa Glomb. The oldest fringe theatre in Seattle, this company is comprised of established actors, writers, and directors. The Project produces contemporary or new works, most often dark comedies. All performers are paid a percentage of the gate after expenses. Watch newspaper callboards and LOFT Hotline for audition notices. STP attends LOFT generals. E-mail: bc269@SCN.org

■ SEX MONK ROCK THEATRE
1715 NW 64th St.
Seattle, WA 98107
(206) 789-6543

    Contact: Bill Sheldon. The theatre is committed to developing individual original works via improvisation techniques. SMRT produces two shows a year. Auditions are on a per show basis; check LOFT Hotline and local newspaper callboards for notices. (Formerly Oxymoron Gesture Factory.)

■ SINING KILUSAN
FILIPINO AMERICAN THEATRE
810 - 18th Ave.
Seattle, WA 98122
(206) 461-4870
Fax: (206) 461-4879

Contact: Timoteo Cordova. Founded in 1989, Sining Kilusan, Seattle's Filipino-American theatre, sponsors two shows per year, as well as three variety shows. Filipinos and Filipino-Americans should send a photo/resume to be considered for the core company (N.B. there are also show-to-show auditions periodically). Check local newspaper callboards for notices. E-mail: 73572.1357@compuserve.com

■ TEATRO LATINO
5203 - 11th Ave. NE
Seattle, WA 98105
(206) 526-2606

Contact: Jose Carillo or Olga Sanchez. In operation since 1992, Seattle's Teatro Latino promotes Latin American performing arts. Teatro Latino has produced a *telenovella*, performed plays in Spanish and developed new works. Ideas for new projects should be submitted to Olga Sanchez.

■ THEATER SCHMEATER
1500 Summit Ave.
Seattle, WA 98122
(206) 324-5621 (ext. 3)

Contact: Anthony Winkler. Theater Schmeater is dedicated to producing great plays, simply, with an

1.4 Fringe

emphasis on both the language of the texts and relevance of the plays for a modern audience. Four to six major productions are done each year, with a varying number of smaller projects interspersed throughout. All productions emphasize the ensemble process, with ongoing training applied to each production. Mainstage actors are paid $100 per show; late-night actors are paid $50. Check LOFT hotline for auditions.

■ **THEATER SIMPLE**
109 N 58th St.
Seattle, WA 98103
(206) 784-8647

Contact: Llysa Holland or Andrew Litzky. Theater Simple is an award-winning, internationally-acclaimed company founded in 1990. It produces three to four shows per season, two of which usually tour schools, communities or international fringe festivals. It accepts new script submissions, and welcomes collaborations. Send headshots/resumes throughout the year. Actors are paid for performances only. Theater Simple attends LOFT generals, and announces auditions in local press callboards and hotlines. E-mail: thsimple@aol.com

■ **THEATRE IN THE WILD**
9758 Arrowsmith Ave. S
Seattle, WA 98118
(206) 286-1842

Contact: Theresa May. The theatre produces plays that "reconnect people with the earth," sometimes outdoors. TITW sponsored the Theatre In An Ecological Age Conference held in Seattle in November 1991, and currently sponsors a theatre education program for elementary-age children. Pay varies from stipend to Arts Paymaster. Consult LOFT Hotline and newspaper callboards for auditions. TITW attends LOFT generals.

1.4 Fringe

■ THEATRE BABYLON
Union Garage,
1418 - 10th Ave.
Seattle, WA. 98102
(206) 860-7726

Contact: D. J. Hamilton. Theatre Babylon is a writers' theater which primarily develops and produces works by local writers and company members. TB produces five to six shows per year, curates a late night series and hosts a series of readings of new works each year. Auditions are held as needed; check local press callboards. E-mail: nebuchnezer @aol.com

■ A THEATRE UNDER THE INFLUENCE
Union Garage
1418 10th Ave.
Seattle, WA. 98122
(206) 467-1840

Contact: Amy Frazier, Artistic Development Director. TUTI produces intriguing — if perhaps less well-known — plays which they feel are unjustly neglected. Each season's choices support a common theme, with emphasis on deep dramaturgical research and artistic, historical and social context. TUTI shares a home with Theatre Babylon, a flexible black box performance space which seats 85 and is available for rentals. All participants get 1 point of profit. The theatre attends LOFT generals; check local press callboards for auditions.

■ URSA MAJOR
906 E. John St. #201
Seattle, WA. 98102
(206) 323-7412

Contact: John Longenbough, Artistic Director. Ursa Major has cultivated a two-fold purpose: finding, cultivating and presenting the best of new plays; and presenting contemporary reinterpretations of the classics,

1.4 Fringe

particularly the plays of the ancient Greeks and those of
Shakespeare. Ursa Major produces two shows per season.
The company profit-shares, casts on a show by show basis,
and attends LOFT generals.

■ **VELVET ELVIS ARTS LOUNGE THEATRE**
107 Occidental
Seattle, WA 98104
(206) 624-8051

Contact: Jeff Frieson, Artistic Director, or Carolyn
Budd, Managing Director. The theatre produces both
contemporary and established off-beat plays with social
value. VEALT is looking for actors willing to take risks.
It produces four to six shows per season, paying a
percentage of box office receipts. Check LOFT Hotlline
and local callboards. VEALT attends LOFT generals. A
LOFT member theatre.

■ **WINDOWLIGHT PRODUCTIONS**
1916 Pike Place #12, Suite 68
Seattle, WA. 98101-1056
(206) 292-0504

Contact: Douglas Staley, Artistic Director. In this,
Windowlight's third full season, the company seeks "to
explore the diversity of human experience by presenting
plays that challenge an audience on a primal and
communal level." Windowlight accepts headshots/
resumes. Actors are paid a stipend of $60 to $150,
depending upon show and cast size. Auditions are
announced in local press callboards.

Oregon

NOTE: For further information about the Portland fringe theatre scene, contact the Portland Area Theatre Alliance at (503) 241-4902. PATA publishes a monthly magazine and conducts biannual general auditions.

■ **ARTIST'S REPERTORY THEATRE**
1111 SW 10th
Portland, OR 97205
(503) 242-2420

■ **COASTER THEATER**
P.O. Box 643
Cannon Beach, OR 97110
(503) 436-1242

■ **ECHO THEATRE**
  DO JUMP DANCE THEATRE CO.
1515 SE 37th
Portland, OR 97214
(503) 231-1232

■ **FIREHOUSE THEATRE**
1436 SW Montgomery
Portland, OR 97201
(503) 244-6367

■ **INTERMEDIATE THEATRE**
  WINNINGSTAD THEATRE
1111 SW Broadway
Portland, OR 97205
(503) 248-4335

■ **INTERSTATE FIREHOUSE CULTURAL CENTER**
(503) 823-2000

1.4 Fringe

■ **LAKEWOOD THEATRE COMPANY**
368 S State
Lake Oswego, OR 97034
(503) 635-3901

■ **MIRACLE THEATRE COMPANY**
2322 SE Yamhill
Portland, OR 97214
(503) 236-0215

■ **MUCK'S CREST PRODUCTIONS**
5000 N Willamette Blvd.
Portland, OR 97203
(503) 283-7450

■ **THE MUSICAL COMPANY**
1436 SW Montgomery
Portland, OR 97201
(503) 224-8730

■ **MYSTIC FRUITCAKE COMPANY**
1530 NE Liberty
Portland, OR 97211-4862
(503) 285-6788

■ **NEW ROSE THEATRE**
904 SW Main
Portland, OR 97205
(503) 222-2487

■ **NORTHWEST THEATRE OF THE DEAF**
(503) 823-2000

■ **OUT-OF-POCKET PRODUCTIONS**
763 NW Jackson
Corvallis, OR 97330
(503) 754-8082

■ **PAULA PRODUCTIONS**
537 SE Ash #21
Portland, OR 97214
(503) 238-9692

■ **PORTLAND ACCESSIBLE THEATRE**
(503) 236-1844

■ **PORTLAND WOMEN'S THEATER CO.**
1728 NE 40th
Portland, OR 97212
(503) 287-7707

■ **SRO PRODUCTIONS**
1530 SW Yamhill
Portland, OR 97205
(503) 226-4026

■ **STARK RAVING THEATRE**
1900 NW 27th
Portland, OR 97210
(503) 222-4349

■ **TRIANGLE PRODUCTIONS**
6 SW 3rd
Portland, OR 97204
(503) 241-3857

■ **TYGRES HEART SHAKESPEARE COMPANY**
710 SW Madison
Portland, OR 97205
(503) 222-9220

1.4 Fringe

Alaska

■ **OUT NORTH THEATRE COMPANY**
P.O. Box 100140
Anchorage, AK 99510
(907) 279-8099

Contact: Gene Dugan, Artistic Director. A seven-year-old Alaskan company with a social conscience and a sense of humor. Conducts workshops with visiting artists, a technical theatre internship program for high school students (with a scholarship program), publishes a quarterly newsletter and produces three shows per season. A LOFT member theater.

COMMUNITY THEATRE

Washington

■ **BAINBRIDGE PERFORMING ARTS**
200 Madison Ave. N
Bainbridge Island, WA 98110
(206) 842-8578
Fax: (206) 842-0195

Contact: Karen Molinari. Bainbridge Performing Arts celebrates its 40th year as a community cultural center, producing four mainstage shows annually, including adult and family dramas, comedies and musicals. Actors are not paid, but may get travel allowances. Directors receive stipends. Auditions are held on a show-by-show basis. Check local press callboards.

■ **BURIEN LITTLE THEATRE**
P.O. Box 48121
Burien, WA 98148
Tel. and fax (206) 242-5180

Contact: Laura Sweeny. In its 16th season, BLT presents at least four major productions between September and May (comedy, mystery, musical or classical), performing at Highline Community Center, 4th Ave. SW and SW 146th St. Each play runs four to six weeks. BLT also produces a four-week Directors' Festival and a play-reading series. Auditions are on a show-by-show basis; check LOFT Hotline and local newspaper callboards.

1.5 Community

■ CAPITOL PLAYHOUSE
612 E 4th Ave.
Olympia, WA 98501
(360) 943-2744

In its tenth year, the Playhouse is known for solid productions of dramas, mysteries, and comedies, with a particular fondness for musicals. It also sponsors Kids At Play classes. Auditions are on a show-by-show basis; call for audition dates.

■ COMMUNITY THEATRE OF BREMERTON
599 Lebo Blvd.
Bremerton, WA 98310
(360) 373-5152

Washington State's second-oldest community theatre group is in its 54th season, with four to six productions a year (comedy, suspense, musicals) between September and June. Each show has a four-weekend run in a 192-seat proscenium theatre. Call for audition information.

■ DRAMA DOCK
P. O. Box 294
Vashon, WA 98070
(206) 463-9640

Founded in 1976, this community group performs three plays from November to July. Cast and crew generally consist of Vashon/Maury island community members, but notices are placed in the Seattle press. Actors are not paid. Directors are solicited each spring from the Puget Sound area, and are paid. Other technical positions receive a stipend.

■ **DRIFTWOOD PLAYERS**
P.O. Box 385
Edmonds, WA 98020
(206) 774-9600
Fax: (206) 672-2827

One of the state's oldest and most respected community theatres is in its 38th season, with at least five productions between September and July. Plays run four to six weekends. Its 223-seat proscenium theatre is located 20 minutes from Seattle in downtown Edmonds, at 950 Main Street. Check newspaper callboards for audition notes.

■ **EMERALD CITY PLAYERS**
11500 38th NE
Seattle, WA 98125
(206) 789-8900

Contact: Ed Poole. Typically, one Broadway musical is produced just before Thanksgiving at Shorecrest Performing Arts Center. Auditions held in late summer; check for announcements in local newspaper callboards.

■ **ENCORE PLAYHOUSE**
P. O. Box 50166
Bellevue, WA 98015
(206) 781-5751

Contact: Lorraine Vagner. Encore Playhouse produces three primarily contemporary plays between the fall and spring, performing at the Sammamish Theatre, at the corner of 140th and Main in Bellevue. It also has a touring program involving Sammamish High School students. Actors paid a small stipend. Auditions are held on a show-by-show basis. Check local newspaper callboards.

1.5 Community

■ **FISHNET THEATRE**
18302 - 72nd Ave. W
Edmonds, WA 98026
(206) 672-8416

Contact: Brent Stainer. Fishnet Theatre is a Christian community theatre. Actors must be Christian to audition. Fishnet produces religious plays in churches, community centers, schools and prisons. Auditions are held March and August; check local newspaper callboards, or call to get on the mailing list.

■ **LANGSTON HUGHES CULTURAL ARTS CENTER**
104 - 17th Ave. S
Seattle, WA 98144
(206) 684-4757
Fax: (206) 233-7149

Contact: Sherry Sparks or Steve Sneed. Langston Hughes needs actors ages 11 to adult for two to three productions annually (summer through winter), as well as instructors for theatre, drama classes, the youth theatre program and cultural arts programs.

■ **NEW SAVOY OPERA**
9100 Roosevelt Way NE #200
Seattle, WA 98122
(206) 325-7903
Fax: (206) 325-7903

Contact: Gwen Lewis. Now in its fifth year, New Savoy produces two Gilbert and Sullivan and one Victorian operetta between November and June. Auditions are on a show-by-show basis; singers and singing actors should check newspaper callboards. New Savoy Performs at the St. Thomas Center in Bothell.

■ **NORTHLAKE PLAYERS**
308 - 4th Ave. S
Kirkland, WA 98033
(206) 822-0171
Fax: (206) 827-1650

Contact: Jackie Mason. Northlake Players produces three shows, September through June. Audition are on a show-by-show basis; check LOFT Hotline and local newspaper callboards. E-mail: bdburke@wolfenet.com

■ **NW SAVOYARDS/PARADOX PLAYERS**
P O Box 8514
Everett, WA 98201
(206) 303-8902

Contact: Janet Erickson. NWS produces two musical comedies, fall and spring, for the Snohomish County communities, performing in the Public Utilities District Auditorium. The core company, Paradox Players, is for hire. Membership in Paradox Players is granted to those who have appeared in at least two shows. For audition information, check the *Seattle Times* and *Everett Herald* for audition notices, or call to be put on the mailing list.

■ **OFF THE WALL PLAYERS**
P. O. Box 731
Monroe, WA 98272
(360) 210-0087

Contact: Corinne Bogan. OTWP produce three shows — musical, mystery and comedy — September through June. Directors receive a stipend. Check *The Seattle Times* and *Everett Herald* for audition notices.

1.5 Community

■ **THE PERFORMANCE CIRCLE**
P.O. Box 4
Gig Harbor, WA 98335
(206) 851-PLAY
Fax: (206) 851-7503

Contact: Roberta Pollock. TPC presents an eight-play season from October to August, three of them outdoor amphitheater productions, as well as touring programs to schools. It is all-volunteer except for directors, who receive a stipend. Check the local newpaper callboards.

■ **PINE NUT PLAYERS**
113 N Lewis
Monroe, WA 98272
(360) 794-7101

Contact: Diane Wilson-Simon. Located east of Seattle in Monroe, Pine Nut produces one to four show per year. Although the theatre is primarily an opportunity for the Monroe community to perform; auditions are announced in the Seattle newspaper callboards.

■ **PUGET SOUND MUSICAL THEATRE**
4434 S 166th St.
Seattle, WA. 98188
(206) 246-1208

Contact: Mary Jean McDonald. Since 1980, PSMT has produced one or two musicals each year between spring and fall. Actors are not paid; directors and technical staff receive a stipend. The company expects strong singing and dancing skills. Auditions are held in April and August; check LOFT Hotline and local newspaper callboards.

■ **RAINIER STAGE COMPANY**
P.O. Box 4
Enumclaw, WA 98022
(360) 825-PLAY

Rainier Stage Company was created six years ago to provide a theatrical opportunity for the talents of area residents. RSC produces two plays per year and sponsors a month-long summer program for kids. Check Enumclaw newspapers, the *Valley Daily News*, the *Pierce County Herald*, or call to get on the mailing list.

■ **REDWOOD THEATRE**
P.O. Box 108
Redmond, WA 98073-0108
(206) 525-3493

Contact: Jay Irwin. Established in 1984, RT "provides quality entertainment to the Eastside and a fun time for actors." Redwood produces three plays per season: comedies, dramas and thrillers. The season runs from September through May. Directors receive $150 stipend. Open auditions; check local press callboards.

■ **SEATTLE MOUNTAINEER PLAYERS**
300 3rd Ave. W
Seattle, WA 98119
(206) 284-6310
Fax: (206) 284-4977

Contact: Mary Duckering. SMP is one of Washington's oldest theatre companies, performing two shows a season in a very impressive space. It participates in the LOFT general auditions. For audition information, watch the newspaper callboards.

1.5 Community

■ **TACOMA LITTLE THEATRE**
210 North "I" St.
Tacoma, WA 98403
(206) 272-2281
Fax: (206) 272-3972

Contact: David Fischer, Managing & Artistic
Director. Founded in 1918, Tacoma Little Theatre is the
oldest community theatre west of Omaha. The company's
300-seat proscenium stage is in Tacoma, 45 minutes from
downtown Seattle. Top-notch professional directors
rehearse and lead volunteers in TLT's six-play season,
which runs from September through June (comedies,
musicals and contemporary dramas). TLT also sponsors
an educational program. Actors are not paid; directors
receive a stipend. To audition, contact the theatre to be
put in the database. Information is sent out three times a
year. Check local press callboards for additional audition
information. E-mail: tlt@nwrain.com

■ **TACOMA MUSICAL PLAYHOUSE**
7116 - 6th Ave.
Tacoma, WA 98406
(206) 565-6867

Contact: Jon Rake. Tacoma Musical Playhouse
conducts workshops throughout the year, and produces
five musicals per year. Auditions are on a show-by-show
basis; check local newspaper callboards, or call to get on
the mailing list.

■ **THEATER ARTS EDUCATION FOUNDATION**
    MAINSTAGE PRODUCTIONS
8601 NE 12th St.
Medina, WA 98039
(206) 450-4043

Contact: Kathleen Higgins, Artistic Director.
Mainstage Productions is a community theater producing
three musicals a year. They use all-volunteer cast and
crew, and announce auditions in local press callboards.

1.5 Community

■ VALLEY COMMUNITY PLAYERS
231½ Main Ave. S
Renton, WA 98055
(206) 226-5190

Contact: Gretchen Swackhamer. This year is the Players' 32nd season presenting comedy, farce, light drama and suspense. Between September and April, four productions will be presented in the 294-seat proscenium theater, located 20 minutes from downtown Seattle. Actors are not paid; directors receive a stipend. Auditions are announced in newspaper callboards; otherwise, call to get on the mailing list.

■ WHIDBEY PLAYHOUSE
P.O. Box 571
Oak Harbor, WA 98277
(360) 679-2237

Contact: Debbie Honebrink. Located two hours from Seattle on beautiful Whidbey Island, the Whidbey Playhouse produces five mainstage shows and several children's shows each year, September through June. All positions are volunteer. Auditions are on a show-by-show basis. Check local press.

<u>Oregon</u>

For information on community theatres in the Portland area, contact the Portland Area Theatre Alliance at (503) 241-4902.

ALTERNATIVE THEATRE

Social/Political

■ **AIDS PREVENTION THEATRE TROUPE**
115 - 15th Ave. E # 201
Seattle, WA. 98112
(206) 322-5258

Contact: Ridgby Biddle. APTT presents two shows a year about AIDS prevention, performed for the mentally ill in mental health facilities and in a youth and school program. Actors are paid a stipend. Auditions are on a show-by-show basis. APTT attends LOFT generals.

■ **BOONDOGGLERS**
P. O. Box 20192
Seattle WA. 98102
(206) 322-5468

Contact: James Jordan. Boondogglers has been performing original, political, "smart-ass" scripted comedy since 1993. The group presents two shows a year and shares all profits. Auditions are on a show-by-show basis. Boondogglers also attends LOFT Generals. E-mail: plaqueura@aol.com

■ **MUNICIPAL LIGHT AND THEATRE**
Contact: Mary Lee Larison. MLT produces subject-specific theatre, creating materials as needed; it performs at events such as the Domestic Violence Conference for city employees. Performances are not open to public. Auditions are on a show-by-show basis. Pay is negotiated per show; the average non-Equity pay is $100 per performance, $10 per hour for rehearsals. Equity contracts also available. Check local newspaper callboards. No

calls or resumes are accepted without request. E-mail: evelyn.chapman@ci.seattle.wa.us

■ PLAYBACK THEATRE NORTHWEST
3820 Meridian Ave.
Seattle, WA 98103
(206) 726-1415

Contact: Becca Brenneman. Founded by Jonathan Fox in 1975, Playback performs improvisational enactments of personal stories provided by the audience. In addition to monthly public performances, the group is available for conferences, staff retreats, and a program to train people in the Playback method. The company pays its performers when possible. Playback maintains a core group for as long as possible, auditioning as individual actors are needed. Auditions are announced in local newspaper callboards and on hotlines.

■ TALK THEATRE
1100 E. Pike
Seattle, WA 98122
(206) 270-8923

Contact: Anne Zanetta. Talk Theatre is a non-profit interactive educational theatre company which tours with a repertoire of scripts, performing for grades K-12, teaching personal body safety and dating skills. It also performs for special-needs population, such as the developmentally disabled. Actors are paid $25 per performance. Auditions are held on a show-by-show basis; check local newspaper callboards.

1.6 Alternative Theatre

<u>Improvisation</u>

■ **FRESH ART ENTERTAINMENT**
603 Stewart St.
Lloyd Bldg. #314
Seattle, WA 98101
(206) 365-8956 (phone and fax)

Contact: David Schwartz. This improvisational comedy troupe has been in existence for five years, most recently as the weekly in-house act Improvus Comicus at the Comedy Underground. Fresh Art performs approximately 100 shows per year. The general public can book "practical jokes" by appointment. Auditions are held once a year; check the local newspaper callboards.

■ **UNEXPECTED PRODUCTIONS**
1428 Post Alley
Seattle, WA 98101
(206) 587-2414

Contact: Keith Dahlgren or Randy Dixon. Unexpected Productions (formerly Theatresports), an improv group, produces improvisational theatre with a competitive edge, and sponsors workshopsl. E-mail: keith@chernobog.wa.com

<u>Miscellanous</u>

■ **BOOK-IT REPERTORY THEATRE**
1219 Westlake Ave. N #301
Seattle, WA 98109
(206) 216-0833
Fax: (206) 216-0723

Contact: Jane Jones. Book-It adapts three to four works of prose literature for the stage, between September and June. The core company of 15, working under the

1.6 Alternative Theatre

Equity umbrella through Arts Paymaster, auditions outside actors on a show-by-show basis. Check local newspaper callboards.

Performance Art

■ **NEW CITY THEATRE AND ARTS CENTER**
1634 - 11th Ave.
Seattle, WA 98122
(206) 323-6801

    Contact: John Kazanjian. Various programs include Theater Zero, a resident professional ensemble; The Second Company, made up of non-union emerging artists; New Dance, with a fall festival of new dance works; Quixotic Film & Video, with weekly showings; Playwrights Festival each January and February; Actors & Directors Festival in July and August; and the Quixotic Café, open morning to afternoon, featuring literary readings, new films by local artists and video programming. Check local listings and callboards.

■ **ON THE BOARDS**
100 Roy St.
Seattle, WA 98119
(206) 325-7902
Fax: (206) 325-7903

    Contact: Mark Murphy, Artistic Director. On the Boards, now in a new permanent space at the old ACT Theatre, is a *presenting* — not producing — venue for new works created by performers in dance, theatre and music. Its 12 Minutes Max series takes place six times a year; call the theatre for the current schedule. The Northwest New Works Festival is an annual presentation of the best in contemporary performance; pick up applications in late summer/early fall. As it is not a producing organization, On the Boards does not accept photos/resumes from individual artists. E-mail: otb@cyberspace.com

1.6 Alternative Theatre

Music Halls/Vaudeville

■ **HOKUM HALL**
7904 35th Ave. SW
Seattle, WA 98126
(206) 937-3613
Fax: (206) 937-0450

Contact: Hokum W. Jeebs, Artistic Director. Hokum
Hall has been in existence for four years as the only
consistently producing Vaudeville venue, with 2 shows a
month year-round. Designated "Best Vaudeville Hall"
by the *Seattle Weekly*, HH also produces Shakespeare.
Titles include *Vaudeville in Flickers*, *The Eightieth Annual
VaudeFest* and *Two Gentlemen of Verona*. Individual acts
are encouraged to audition. Check newspaper callboards.
E-mail: hwjeebs@aol.com

Stand-Up Comedy

■ **GIGGLES**
5220 Roosevelt Way NE
Seattle, WA 98105
(206) 526-5347

Contact: Bob or Brad Davis. Located in the University
District, Giggles Comedy Club presents headliners from
out of town with local opening acts Thursday through
Sunday. New talent can do an unpaid "guest set" which
can lead to MC or Opening Act bookings for pay.

1.6 Alternative Theatre

■ **SWANNIE'S/THE COMEDY UNDERGROUND**
222 S. Main St.
Seattle, WA 98104
(206) 782-8470

    Contact: Ron Reid. Although headliners are booked by Fox Productions in San Francisco, local talent may participate in Monday and Tuesday's open mic nights by calling Ron Reid or signing in at 7:30 p.m. for possible guest sets and opening spots. (See 3.1 Talent Agents.)

<u>Oregon</u>

■ **TOAD CITY PRODUCTIONS**
P. O. Box 731
Portland, OR 97207
(503) 736-1027

    Contact: Adrienne Flagg. Toad City specializes in cabaret and improvisation, with an emphasis on Commedia dell' Arte. One to five productions per year are cast through the PATA generals, and pay a small stipend.

THEATRE FESTIVALS

Washington & British Columbia

■ COMEDY COMPETITION
719 N 78th St.
Seattle, WA 98103
(206) 782-8470

Contact: Ron Reid. This month-long comedy competition, ending the week after Thanksgiving, is for professional stand-up comedians only. The prize is $10,000. Auditions are announced in newspaper callboards. Prospective participants may send a videotape if they are unavailable for live audition.

■ NEW CITY PLAYWRIGHTS' FESTIVAL
(206) 323-6801

Contact: Karen Uffelman. The Festival is New City Theatre's annual fall showcase for new works by Northwest playwrights. Auditions are held during the first two weeks in August. Each production gets a single performance, and is brought back for a brief return engagement if designated as among "The Best of the Fest." For the benefit of Equity performers, the festival operates under the Equity Staged Reading Code.

■ PORTLAND REP PLAYWRIGHTS FESTIVAL
(503) 224-4491

Contact: Dennis Bigelow. Portland Rep's juried Playwrights Festival runs for two weeks in September. Submissions are due in early January. Scripts must be approximately 30 minutes. (See 1.2 Equity Theatre.)

■ **SEATTLE FRINGE FESTIVAL**
P.O. Box 20730
Seattle, WA 98102
(206) 325-5446

Contact: Michael Olich. The annual Seattle Fringe Festival takes place in March on Capitol Hill. Approximately 75 theatre companies participate, presenting a diverse and electric range of plays, musical theatre, movement, improvisation and other performance styles at affordable prices.

The Festival provides performance venues, lights and sound for three to five performances per participant, as well as general advertising and promotion; participants are responsible for production-related royalties and marketing, rehearsal space and other production needs. There is a $350 application fee; the festival returns an artistic fee(based on audience attendance) to all participants. SSF is non-juried, so participation is on a first come, first served basis. Applications are due in September.

■ **SKAGIT VALLEY NEW PLAY FESTIVAL**
2405 College Way
Mt. Vernon, WA 98273
(360) 416-7723

Contact: Andy Friedlander. This annual festival takes place the last two weekends in June. The Festival is looking for short plays that run up to 30 minutes, monologues and other short scripts. Playwrights receive a nominal royalty. Actors are all local college students. Deadline for submission: December 1.

1.7 Festivals

■ **VANCOUVER FRINGE FESTIVAL**
First Vancouver Theatre Space Society
#18-2414 Main St.
Vancouver, B.C., CANADA V5T 3E3
(604) 873-3646
Fax: (604) 873-4231

In its thirteenth year of existence, the festival's attendance has grown to over 30,000. The festival presents more than 500 performances of over 100 different productions (from across Canada, the US and the world) from noon to midnight over eleven days. The festival is held in September. Participation is non-juried, "first come, first served" basis; there is an entry fee.

■ **VICTORIA FRINGE FESTIVAL**
Intrepid Theatre Company
620 View St. #602
Victoria, B.C., CANADA V8W 1J6
(604) 383-2663

Contact: Tammy Issacson. This festival generally hosts 350 performances by 55 companies. Applications are available in mid-December, and are accepted on a first come, first served basis. Application fee is $360 Canadian.

SUMMER STOCK

The Northwest

Washington

■ **CAMLANN MEDIEVAL FAIRE**
10320 Kelly Rd. NE
Carnation, WA 98014
(206) 788-1353

Faire Coordinator: Roger Shell. This mid-summer Medieval Faire has costumed characters speaking memorized scripts, and also improvising. Open weekends in July and August, the Faire requires actors with improv skills and an interest in medieval history. Rehearsals are in Seattle; the Faire site is located 35 minutes from downtown Seattle. All positions are paid. Auditions are held in April/May; watch for newspaper audition notices, or call the Faire.

■ **COLUMBIA THEATRE**
  FOR THE PERFORMING ARTS
  THE STAGE COMPANY
1231 Vandercook
Longview, WA. 98632
(360) 423-1011
Fax: (360) 423-8626

Contact: James Murphy. CTPA is located in a 1,000-seat historic vaudeville theatre built in 1925. It will produce *Oklahoma* in 1997; rehearsals begin in June for July performances. Auditions are in April and through the PATA generals. Check Portland newspaper callboards. Pay ranges from a $100 stipend to Equity minimum.

N.B. Actors looking for Summer Shakespeare should see 1.11 Shakespeare.

1.8 Summer Stock

■ **LAUGHING HORSE SUMMER THEATRE**
P.O. Box 1412
Ellensburg, WA 98926
(509) 963-3400
Fax: (509) 963-1767

Contact: Brenda Hubbard, Artistic Director.
Laughing Horse produces four non-musicals in repertory
from June to August at Central Washington University.
The theatre hires eight to twelve performers, three
directors and several designer/technical interns each
season. Submissions for employment should be sent by
December 15. Send photo/resume by mid-January.
Auditions will be held in Seattle, Portland and Ellensburg
in early spring, and are open to all, not just students at
CSU. Pay varies from stipends for student interns to
Equity scale. No phone calls, please.

■ **SEATTLE GILBERT & SULLIVAN SOCIETY**
800 Mercer St. #B
Seattle, WA 98109
(206) 682-0796

Contact Jon Palmason. The Society, one of the
nation's oldest companies devoted exclusively to Gilbert
& Sullivan, will celebrate its 44th season in 1997 with a
production of *Iolanthe*. Its annual all-volunteer production
will be held in July at the Bagley Wright Theatre (11
performances total). Auditions are in February; rehearsals
begin in March. Check local newspaper callboards.

■ **SNOQUALMIE FALLS FOREST THEATRE**
P.O. Box 516
Bellevue, WA 98009
(206) 222-7044

Contact: Roger Westberg. The company hosts one
production of family fare between June and September.
Its large, outdoor amphitheater is located in Fall City, 45
minutes from downtown Seattle. Shows run for four

weekends, or twelve performances. Larger musicals run for six weeks. Actors are paid between $300 and $400 a show. For the Youth Theater, musicians and other staff positions are paid, but actors are not. Directors are hired on a show-by-show basis. Send photo/resumes year-round. Auditions are held in April/May; rehearsals are held either in Seattle or Bellevue. Check local newspaper callboards and hotlines.

■ **SNOQUALMIE FALLS YOUTH THEATRE**

Same as above. Contact: Roger Westberg, Director. SFYT is committed to providing teens with the opportunity to work in theatre. They produce one musical in August. Call for casting information.

Oregon

■ **UNIVERSITY OF PORTLAND THEATRE/**
MUCKS' CREST PRODUCTIONS
5000 N Willamette Blvd.
Portland, OR. 97203
(503) 283-7228
Fax: (503) 283-7399

Contact: Roger Doyle, Department Chair. Mucks Crest Productions presents a Gilbert & Sullivan operetta in June. Actors are paid a stipend. Auditions are open to actors outside the university; check Portland papers January/February. Mucks' Crest is a member of PATA. E-mail: reid@uofport.edu Web site: http://www.uofport.edu

1.8 Summer Stock

Idaho

■ **COEUR D'ALENE SUMMER THEATRE**
P. O. Box 2492
Coeur d'Alene, ID 83816
(208) 769-7780
Fax: (208) 667-1150

Contact: Roger Welch, Artistic Director. Located in scenic Idaho, Coeur d'Alene summer theatre produces four Broadway musicals "as they were meant to be seen" running in July and August. Non-union pay is $150 to $200 a week, plus housing. Auditions are held in Seattle in February. Check Seattle newspaper callboards and hotlines.

■ **IDAHO REPERTORY THEATRE COMPANY**
Hartung Theatre
University of Idaho
Moscow, ID 83843
(208) 885-6465

Contact: Charles Ney, Artistic Director. The University of Idaho's summer repertory company, now in its 44th year, stages four productions in rotating repertory in June and July. Acting and technical auditions are held at the Northwest Drama Conference Summer Auditions in February. Additional auditions are held at the University of Texas at Austin, Southern Methodist University in Dallas and in the Seattle area. Contact IRTC in January for additional information and dates.

Montana

■ **MONTANA SHAKESPEARE IN THE PARKS**
Montana State University
Dept. of Media and Theatre Arts
Bozeman, MT 59717-0400
(406)9 94-3901
Fax : (406) 994-4591

Producer/Artistic Director: Joel Jahnke. The company, co-sponsored by the university, tours two summer productions in rotating repertory throughout Montana. All performances are outdoor; the cast is expected to handle technical duties. Starting pay for first-year company members is $225 to 250 per week. Room and board are provided for the 12-week tour. Send photo/ resume by February first; call for possible Seattle auditions, generally held in January/February. Designers/technical positions are available through late May/June. Send resume. Check Seattle newspaper callboards and the company's web site for audition notices. E-mail: aftjj@msu.oscs.montana.edu   Web site: http:// www.montana.edu/2wwwxs/monshakes.html

■ **VIRGINIA CITY PLAYERS**
P.O. Box 63
Virginia City, MT 59755
(206) 782-3646

Contact: B. J. Douglas. Located in an historic gold rush town, Virginia City Players has been in operation since 1947 and specializes in 19th-century plays and vaudeville. They produce three shows between June and Labor Day. The nine to twelve company members perform seven times a week. Salary is $210 a week plus room and two meals a day. Technical positions are available. Auditions are held in early spring; check newspaper callboards, LOFT Hotline or call.

1.8 Summer Stock

■ **BIGFORK SUMMER PLAYHOUSE**
P.O. Box 456
Bigfork, MT 59911
(406) 837-6843

Producer: Donald Thomson. Bigfork is one of Montana's oldest repertory companies. Between the end of May and Labor Day, four musicals and one play are performed in repertory at a 425-seat, open proscenium theatre. Actors are paid $185 per week plus dormitory accommodations with kitchen and laundry facilities. Director, designer and staff salaries are negotiable. Bigfork is especially interested in college-age musical theatre performers. Send videotape, photo/resume and two letters of reference by March 15th. Producers attend auditions at the Northwest Theatre Conference, Rocky Mountain Theatre Conference, Mid-America Conference, SETC, and Midwest auditions in St. Louis and SCETA in California.

TOURING COMPANIES

The Northwest & National

■ **IT'S A MYSTERY**
P.O. Box 27022
Seattle, WA 98125
(206) 783-4102
Fax: (206) 486-6479

Contact: Daryl Strandlien. It's A Mystery produces 200 murder mystery events annually throughout the Northwest and British Columbia. Events are individually tailored for each audience. Pay is $50 to $85 per performance, with minimal rehearsals. The company is looking for actors, usually in their 30's, with good improvisational skills, but will consider all types. Although the company is busy at all times of the year, there is a big flurry of activity during the winter holiday season, so if actors wish to work those shows, they should submit photo/resumes in August. However, the company is always looking for new people. Send photo/resume.

■ **MISSOULA CHILDREN'S THEATRE**
221 E Front
Missoula, MT 59802
(406) 728-1911

Associate Artistic Director: Don Kukla. The Missoula Children's Theatre is a nonprofit, professional touring company in operation since 1973. It establishes short acting residencies in schools and community centers throughout the U.S., Canada, Guam and Singapore. MCT demands strong acting, directing, and teaching skills; it requires three letters of recommendation and two references. Participants receive a salary and health benefits. Auditions are held in February/ March in several Northwest cities; video auditions are also possible.

1.9 Touring Companies

■ **MOBILE OUTREACH BUNCH**
(206) 443-2210
> (*See* Seattle Repertory Theatre in 1.2 Equity Theatre.)

■ **THE MONTANA REP** (URTA)
c/o University of Montana Drama Dept.
Missoula, MT 59812
(406) 243-6809

Artistic Director: Mary Ann Riddle. The Montana Rep is a professional touring company based in Missoula at the University of Montana. The company travels by van and truck throughout the West, performing two shows in repertory.

The ensemble tours for four months, with rehearsals beginning in December. Equity members are paid $575/week plus per diem while on the road. Send photo and resume to Artistic Director by mid-May; auditions will follow. The company is also seeking stage managers.

■ **ON STAGE ALASKA**
300 Elliott Ave. W
Seattle, WA 98119
(206) 281-5181

Contact: Kim Anderson. OSA does promotional sales tours, promoting Alaska cruise ship vacations. Sponsored by a major cruise ship company, the production consists of sketches depicting historical Alaskan figures. Auditions are held in July; tours begin in the fall.

The six-month road tour demands experience, production savvy, and plenty of stamina. Pay is $1,500 per month, plus per diem.

1.9 Touring Companies

■ **OPEN DOOR THEATRE**
917 - 134th St. SW #A6
Everett, WA 98204
(206) 787-9304
Fax: (206) 734-1440

Artistic Director: Hal Ryder. This nonprofit educational troupe, founded in 1983, tours Snohomish, Pierce and King County and national classrooms between September and June. Its performances, acclaimed by state and federal educators, are designed to help children and youth learn sexual abuse prevention skills.

The company of fourteen performers (Equity and non-Equity under PP contract) tours three shows aimed at pre-school through high school. Auditions for the 10-month season are held in spring. Call in late April for audition information; also check Equity & LOFT Hotlines. Pay is $25 to $35 per performance for up to three shows a day. Transportation and meals for out-of-state shows can be provided. Open Door encourages the participation of minorities.

■ **SMALL CHANGE ORIGINAL THEATRE**
212 Third Ave. N #205
Minneapolis, MN 55401
(800) 858-3999
Fax: (612) 341-2277

Contact: Heidi Bush-Gallanar. SCOT is a national educational touring company producing 30 to 40 original scripts per year for grades K-12. Pay is $320 per week to non-union performers, plus per diem on tour and traveling expenses. The theatre conducts Seattle auditions in November and December for spring tours in the Puget Sound Area. Send picture/resume.

CABARET, DINNER & MYSTERY THEATRE

Washington

Dinner Theatre

■ **AUBURN AVENUE DINNER THEATRE AND OPRY HOUSE**
10 Auburn Ave.
Auburn, WA 98002
(206) 833-5678
Fax: (206) 833-5648

Contact: Deanna Robinson. Western Washington's oldest, continuous dinner theatre makes its home in a sprawling ex-vaudeville house south of Seattle. First weekend of every month features a country-opry show; the other weekends feature plays and musicals. Send resume; actors and directors are paid a stipend.

Cabaret

■ **CABARET DE PARIS**
1333 Fourth Ave.
Seattle, WA 98101
(206) 935-4225

Contact: David Hunter Koch. This professional cabaret is dedicated to creating and developing small stage musical theatre. It presents eight to ten new shows a year at the Crepe de Paris Restaurant, downtown. Casts are small: two to six performers and a musical director. The Cabaret pays per week. General auditions for experienced union or non-union stage singers with musical comedy for cabaret background are held in February; call for an appointment.

■ **VARIETY PLUS**
223 NE 175th
Shoreline, WA 98155
(206) 368-8386

Contact: Angela Rinaldi. Variety Plus performs three to five cabaret and vaudeville shows per season. Non-union pay for adults is $30 to $50 per show. Group auditions are held for kids in the fall; check LOFT hotline and newspaper callboards. Adult auditions are on a show-by-show basis.

Mystery Theatre

■ **MYSTERY CAFÉ**
4105 E Madison, Suite 310
Seattle, WA 98112
(206) 324-8895
Fax: 324-8870

Mystery Café is an interactive mystery dinner theatre "where murder is always on the menu." Performances are on Friday and Saturday nights, with a multi-course dinner served by the actors between acts; there are also touring productions. Actors have three-month contracts, with non-union pay.

Oregon

Cabaret

■ **ACTOR'S CABARET OF EUGENE**
996 Willamette
Eugene, OR 97401
(541) 683-4368

This year-round professional cabaret schedules off-Broadway-style productions for local restaurants and

1.10 Cabaret/Dinner

theatres.   Actor's Cabaret is interested in experienced
cabaret and musical theatre performers. There are usually
11 to 15 performances per show, 10 to 15 shows per year.
Cast is all-volunteer. Producing and Artistic Director, Jim
Roberts, auditions show-by-show for two to four
productions per year; notices are usually listed in
newspapers.

■ **OREGON CABARET THEATRE**
P.O. Box 1149
Ashland, OR 97520
(541) 488-2902
Fax: (541) 488-8795

   Contact: James Giancarlo. OCT, a professional non-
equity theatre in Ashland, produces a season of primarily
musicals between February and December, and draws
heavily on actor/singers from Portland and Seattle. Send
a photo/resume in advance of the December/January
auditions; experienced performers are also invited to call
for a spot audition. Contract runs 6 to 16 weeks.

Dinner Theatre

■ **SYLVIA'S CLASS ACT DINNER THEATRE**
5115 NE Sandy Blvd.
Portland, OR 97213
(503) 288-6928
Fax: (503) 288-2103

   Contact: Patti Gosser. Sylvia's produces four shows
between September and August, usually light comedies
and revues. Pays for a 30-50 non-union performance run,
depending on size, complexity and importance of role.
Auditions are on a show-to-show basis; check Portland
newspaper callboards.

1.10 Cabaret/Dinner

Mystery Theatre

■ **EDDIE MAY MYSTERIES**
12890 SW Village Park Lane
Tigard, OR 97223
(503) 524-4366
Fax: (503) 590-8314

Contact: Genevieve Jones, Associate Producer. Eddie May Mysteries produces 12 dinner/mystery shows per year. Actors are paid $35 to $40 per show. EMM participates in PATA general auditions in early October; call for dates. Send photo/resume.

SHAKESPEARE

Summary

Summer

■ WILLIE THE SHAKES

(See Brown Bag Theatre in 1.3 Non-Union Professional.)

■ GREENSTAGE
5911 Airport Way S
Seattle, WA 98108
(206) 935-5606

Contact: Tony Discoll or Ken Holmes. Performing primarily in Seattle's parks, Greenstage produces three to four shows per year: one indoor show in the spring is remounted in the summer; the remaining shows tour different Seattle Parks. With a heavy performance commitment, up to 26 performances, actors get a base pay plus a percentage of the profits. Since the mission of the theatre is to make Shakespeare accessible, the shows are free to the public; revenue is generated by passing the hat.

■ IDAHO SHAKESPEARE FESTIVAL (SPT)
P.O. Box 9365
Boise, ID 83707
(208) 336-9221

Contact: Charles Fee, Artistic Director. Actors, designers, technicians and interns come from all over the country to work for this well-established Northwest theatre company. Four outdoor amphitheater production between June and mid-September. Operating under a small professional theatre Equity contract, Idaho Shakespeare hires at least a dozen non-union performers, paying $1,300 to $1,500 for the season plus housing; kitchen facilities are provided. Send photo/resume to

artistic director by mid-January. An open call is held soon
after in Seattle.

■ **MONTANA SHAKESPEARE IN THE PARKS**
Montana State University
Dept. of Media & Theatre Arts
Bozeman, MT 59717-0400
(406) 994-3901
Fax: (406) 994-4591

Contact: Joel Jahnke, Producer and Artistic Director.
The company, sponsored by Montana State University,
tours two summer productions in rotating repertory
throughout Montana. All performances are outdoors.
Starting pay is $225 to $250 per week; room and board
are provided during the 12 weeks of tour. The cast is
expected to handle tech duties as well. Send photo/
resume by February first. Call or e-mail for possible Seattle
auditions, generally held in January/ February. Designer
and technical positions are available through late May and
June. Check Seattle hotlines, newspaper callboards and
the web site (http://www.montana.edu/2wwwxs/
monshakes.html). E-mail: aftjj@msu.oscs.montana.edu

■ **WASHINGTON SHAKESPEARE FESTIVAL**
P.O. Box 1501
Olympia, WA 98507
(360) 943-9492

Contact: James A. Van Leishout. Founded in 1985,
Washington Shakespeare Festival performs in the
Washington Center for the Performing Arts, Stage 2, every
spring and summer. WSF offers two musicals or light
comedies in the spring and one non-Shakespeare and two
Shakespeare in the summer. Actors make between $400
and $500 per season, plus housing and/or local travel.
Director, set designer and costumer are paid $1,000; stage
managers get $500 per show. Actors with classical training
and experience should send a photo/resume by March
first to the artistic director, and attend an open call by

1.11 Shakespeare

appointment. Actors resident outside the area may attend Northwest Drama Conference Auditions. (See 1.13 Theatre Organizations.)

■ WOODEN "O" THEATRE PRODUCTIONS
2440 - 64th Ave. SE
Mercer Island, WA 98040
(206) 541-2371

Contact: George Mount. Founded four years ago, Wooden "O" is a classical repertory company producing free outdoor Shakespeare at Luther Burbank Theatre on Mercer Island. This year's director is planning *A Midsummer Night's Dream*, with music. Actors are paid a stipend of $100 for the run. Actors, especially those who can sing, should send a photo/resume; check callboards and hotlines in early May for audition times.

Year-round

■ NORTHWEST SHAKESPEARE ENSEMBLE
2114 Seventh Ave. W #1
Seattle, WA 98119
(206) 784-8521

Contact: Helen Murray. NWSE is a small theatre company with an emphasis on classical theatre, education and a commitment to providing audiences access to the classics at reasonable prices. It produces three shows per season. NWSE auditions on a show-by-show basis, and attends LOFT Generals. It pays a stipend based on box office receipts and cast size.

■ OREGON SHAKESPEARE FESTIVAL (LORT B)

(See 1.2 Equity Theatre.)

1.11 Shakespeare

■ **SEATTLE SHAKESPEARE FESTIVAL** (SPT/TYA)
1904 Third Ave. #327
Seattle, WA 98101-1183
(206) 467-6283
Fax: (206) 784-5177

Contact: Benji Bittle, Executive Director. SSF is a non-profit, resident, professional Shakespeare company. Producing three shows a season, plus an outdoor summer show at the Seattle Center. Send a photo and resume by April and check the Equity hotline and local newspaper callboards for general audition notices. Thirty non-Equity positions are filled each season. The company also sponsors a summer touring education program which features smaller, more streamlined productions. Tours last for three months, and generally pay $200-$300 per week, plus expenses. Web site: http://www.seanet.com/ ~ssf/ E-mail: ssf@ssf.seanet.com

THEATRE INTERNSHIPS

<u>Washington</u>

■ **A CONTEMPORARY THEATRE**
(206) 285-3220

Offers a limited number of administrative and production internships; most include a stipend. For information about administrative internships, contact Jim Verdery. (See 1.2 Equity.)

■ **THE BATHHOUSE THEATRE**
(206) 524-3608

Offers internships in all areas of theatre; write or call for information. (See 1.2 Equity.)

■ **THE EMPTY SPACE THEATRE**
(206) 547-7633

Offers unpaid internships in acting, production, public relations, marketing, publications, development, fundraising and literary management. Write to the Internship Coordinator for an application. (See 1.2 Equity.)

■ **THE GROUP THEATRE**
(206) 441-9480

Seasonal or per show internships are available. Contact: for technical, Rex Carleton; for administrative, Rosa Morgan; and for acting, José Carrasquillo. All interns are paid a stipend. (See 1.2 Equity.)

1.12 Internships

■ INTIMAN THEATRE
(206) 269-1901

Offers internships in theatre administration, marketing, office management and production. Excellent opportunities for advancement. Call or write Internship Coordinator.

Intiman also offers "journeymanships" in acting, directing, and both acting and directing. Send a letter of interest to Associate Director, Victor Pappas. For all other internships, call company manager, Jim Loder. (See 1.2 Equity.)

■ NEW CITY THEATRE
(206) 323-6801

Occasional production internships are advertised show-by-show in area newspapers. (See 1.2 Equity.)

■ SEATTLE CHILDREN'S THEATRE
(206) 443-0807

Two or three internships, a combination of arts administration and teaching, are available each summer in the Education Department. They are approximately eight weeks long; a stipend is possible. Contact Dr. Christine Tanner, Education Director, for information. Internships are also available in marketing/public relations, administration, production and technical production. Contact Kathy Alm. (See 1.2 Equity.)

■ SEATTLE REPERTORY THEATRE
(206) 443-2210

The Rep's Professional Arts Training Program offers practical experience in a dozen areas of theatre production and administration. Interns receive a limited stipend; academic credit can be arranged. Applicant deadline is April 15; call for an application. (See 1.2 Equity.)

1.12 Internships

■ **SEATTLE SHAKESPEARE FESTIVAL**
(206) 467-6283

Unpaid apprenticeships are available for high school students. (See 1.2 Equity.)

■ **STUDIO EAST**
(206) 827-3123

Internships in production, technical theatre, marketing and fund-raising are offered year-round in eight- to twelve-week periods. Contact Jennifer Reif, Educational Director.

■ **TACOMA ACTORS GUILD**
(206) 272-3107

Offers internships in all areas: technical, administrative, stage management and acting. Contact Kamella Tate for information. (See 1.2 Equity.)

■ **WASHINGTON SHAKESPEARE FESTIVAL**
(360) 943-9492

Offers interships in technical theatre and acting for college students and recent graduates. Pay varies; housing is sometimes provided.

Oregon

■ **PORTLAND REPERTORY THEATRE**
(503) 224-9221 ext. 200

Offers administrative and production internships. Contact Joan Hartzell. (See 1.2 Equity.)

THEATRE ORGANIZATIONS

Washington

■ **ACTORS' EQUITY ASSOCIATION**
(206) 637-7332
Fax: (206) 823-9799

Actor's Equity Association, AEA, is the national labor union representing professional stage actors and stage managers. The Northwest has over 400 members, and is one of the dozen largest AEA memberships in the country.

At the present time, AEA does not have an office in the Northwest. However, a Seattle Area Equity Liaison Committee has been created to act as a conduit between membership and the Equity offices. The committee members, who are volunteers, are not official representatives of the union, and cannot negotiate or dictate policy. They operate a member hotline, accessible from 5 p.m. to 8 a.m. Monday through Friday and all day Saturday and Sunday.

For information about contracts or other Equity-related questions, call the Hotline to get the current Seattle Liaison contact number, or call Equity's offices in Los Angeles (213-462-2334) or New York (212-869-8530).

■ **ALLIED ARTS OF SEATTLE**
105 S Main St. #201
Seattle, WA 98104
(206) 624-0432
Fax: (206) 624-0433

Allied Arts of Seattle, founded in 1954, is a nonprofit membership organization which advocates urban design and planning, historic preservation, and the arts in Seattle. The Metropolitan Arts Committee of Allied Arts works on issues affecting the performing and visual arts, including public support, legal issues and facility needs.

1.13 Theatre Organizations

■ AMERICAN GUILD OF MUSICAL ARTISTS
11021 NE 123rd Lane #C116
Kirkland, WA 98034
(206) 820-2999
Fax: (206) 823-9799

Contact: Carolyn Carpp, Northwest Representative.
AGMA is the national labor union representing opera and
ballet performers, stage managers, directors and
choreographers. In the Northwest, AGMA has contracts
with Seattle Opera, Portland Opera and Pacific Northwest
Ballet.

While AGMA's national office is in New York, the
Northwest does have a paid AGMA Representative who
negotiates contracts and is available to answer questions.

■ ARTSPACE
P.O. Box 1843
Seattle, WA 98111-1843
(206) 442-9365

Artspace is a nonprofit tax exempt [501(c)(3)]
corporation working to develop living/working space for
low-income artists and nonprofit arts organizations in the
Seattle area.

■ ARTS PAYMASTER
(206) 324-7700

Contact: Ben Rankin. Arts Paymaster provides
business services such as payroll and financial
management for small theatres. Headed by Ben Rankin,
who has eight years' experience in arts administration,
Arts Paymaster's main function is to administer Equity's
SPT umbrella contract for fringe (or non-Equity) theatres.
Seattle is one of the few cities where fringe theatres can
employ Equity actors through a modified SPT contract
without signing a binding contract.

1.13 Theatre Organizations

■ DRAMATISTS & ACTORS MEETING NOW
505 Belmont Ave. E #906
Seattle, WA 98102
(206) 726-9814

Contact: Henry Coffin. Formerly the Playwrights Co-op, DAMN is a group of actors and playwrights holding private play readings to workshop plays. Call for more information.

■ THE GOLIATH PROJECT
P.O. Box 31612
Seattle, WA 98103
(206) 547-6331

Contact: William Scott. This nonprofit cultural and educational group is committed to promoting understanding of Middle Eastern cultures and issues. Goliath is a focal point for Middle Eastern performing arts groups in the Northwest, and produces theatre, music, and dance works throughout the year. The group also helps cast a variety of arts functions.

■ LEAGUE OF FRINGE THEATERS
P.O. Box 20730
Seattle, WA 98102
(206) 637-7373

The League of Fringe Theatres (LOFT) promotes the interests of Seattle's fringe theatres. It sponsors a hotline, and general auditions for member companies every fall.

■ NORTHWEST PLAYWRIGHTS' GUILD
P.O. Box 95259   408 SW Second Ave. #427
Seattle, WA 98145   Portland, OR 97204
(206) 298-9361   (503) 244-1606

The NWPG supports playwrights throughout the Northwest in the development of new plays by providing forums for the exchange of information and ideas about play writing. Ongoing projects include quarterly

1.13 Theatre Organizations

newsletters, workshops with nationally recognized playwrights and play readings. The Washington branch maintains a resume file of actors and directors interested in participating in their Playwrights-in-Progress series of readings. Resumes can be sent to the Seattle address above, Attn.: PIP Coordinator. The Oregon branch contact is Michael Whelan.

■ REACT (REGIONAL EQUITY ACTORS)
(206) 782-1958

The organization arranges for performers to audition for the artistic directors of some of the nation's leading regional theatre companies. The nonprofit, all-volunteer program charges between $10 and $12 to defray the visitor's traveling expenses, and arranges audition slots on a first come, first served basis (Equity members and Equity membership candidates have priority).

■ U.S. INSTITUTE FOR THEATRE TECHNOLOGY
Pacific Northwest Section
P.O. Box 19722
Seattle, WA 98109

The Seattle area branch of the USITT publishes a newsletter, presents seminars, coordinates social functions and relays information from the national headquarters of the country's major organization for technical theatre personnel.

■ WASHINGTON ALLIANCE FOR THEATRE EDUCATION (W.A.T.E.)
1926 NE 98th Loop
Vancouver, WA 98664
(206) 848-5927

Contact: Linda Belt. W.A.T.E. is a statewide organization of high-school theatre educators. It sponsors theatre festivals and workshops on a regular basis, and publishes a quarterly newsletter, *The Spotlight*.

1.13 Theatre Organizations

Oregon

■ **ARTS NORTHWEST**
P.O. Box 443
West Linn, OR 97068-443
(503) 650-4996
Fax: (503) 650-4883

Contact: Jack Alotto. Formerly Pacific Northwest Arts Presenter, Arts Northwest is a nonprofit networking group that brings nonprofit presenting groups together with touring actors from throughout the five-state Northwest and British Columbia area (promoting regional "block booking" in the process). In its sixteenth year, Arts Northwest is sponsored by several Northwest state arts commissions. A directory and bimonthly newsletter are available. Arts Northwest produces the Northwest Booking Conference.

■ **NORTHWEST DRAMA CONFERENCE AUDITIONS**
Attn: Mark Kuntz
Department of Theatre Arts
Eastern Oregon State College
LaGrand, OR 97850
(541) 962-3797
Fax: (541) 962-3596

A number of summer theatres and graduate programs are represented at the auditions held at the annual Northwest Drama Conference in February. Audition fee: $5 for summer theatre program, $5 for graduate programs, $8 for both. For information and application form, write by December first.

1.13 Theatre Organizations

■ **NORTHWEST PLAYWRIGHTS' GUILD
PORTLAND**

(See above under Washington organizations.)

■ **PATA
(PORTLAND AREA THEATRE ALLIANCE)**
c/o Fine Arts Building
1017 SW Morrison #105
Portland, OR 97205
(503) 241-4902

Contact: Julie Stewart. PATA is a coalition of Equity
and non-Equity theatres and individuals in Portland. Now
in its sixth year, the group publishes a monthly magazine,
sponsors workshops and seminars, and in spring and fall
conducts open auditions for the city's leading resident and
freelance directors. Membership is $20 a year (the PATA
card also gets space-available discounts at most Equity
and non-Equity theatres).

2

The Actor's Craft

ACTING COACHES/STAGE

Seatttle

■ **RICHARD BRESTOFF**   **(206) 284-5720**

Richard Brestoff, one of Seattle's newest acting teachers, coaches both for stage and camera auditions and general acting. With an M.F.A in acting from New York University, he often prepares students for conservatory auditions. Brestoff has been in Seattle for four years and has numerous national stage credits, including Seattle Rep, Lincoln Center, and the Zephyr in L.A., as well as 18 years in Hollywood. He teaches at Westlake Actor's Center.

■ **LANI BROCKMAN**   **(206) 827-3123**
(EQUITY, SAG)

Private coaching. Brockman trained at Circle In The Square Theatre in NYC, and is currently artistic director at Studio East. She is an excellent resource for audition pieces, and excels in getting that "old standard" rejuvenated and ready for that last-minute time slot.

■ **TED D'ARMS**   **(206) 282-2254**
(EQUITY, SAG, AFTRA)

Audition coaching, by interview only. An actor/director, D'Arms has been a part of the regional theatre scene for 30 years. He studied with Hagen and Katsellas in New York, and taught at Harvard, the University of Washington and Cornish College of the Arts.

2.1 Acting Coaches/Stage

■ TONI DOUGLASS   (206) 244-7558
(Equity, AFTRA)

Private audition coaching. Douglass is an actor/director/playwright whose regional acting credits include Intiman, ACT, Empty Space, Seattle Group Theatre, Tacoma Actors Guild and Southcoast Repertory Co. A playwright with 15 published plays to her credit, Douglass also writes custom audition pieces, which she will coach to performance level.

■ MARY EWALD   (206) 324-7217
(Equity, SAG, AFTRA)

Mary Ewald, resident artist at New City/Theatre Zero, does individual coaching and workshops with both classical and contemporary material. She has been a professional actress for 16 years and has performed at all of the Seattle major theatres, as well as companies on both coasts.

■ RITA GIOMI   (206) 784-6065

Audition workshops and private coaching. Giomi is a recognized Seattle director with an MFA in directing, and 13 years of professional experience at many of the Northwest's leading Equity houses. Giomi's audition workshops are well attended.

■ ALTHEA HUKARI   (206) 323-7499

Althea Hukari has taught acting at Freehold Theatre lab since 1991. She has worked with beginning and professional actors as a coach for auditions and film work. Her highly physical approach specializes in clarifying action, deepening emotional connection to the text and releasing habitual blocks which inhibit full and authentic expression.

2.1 Acting Coaches/Stage

■ **VICTOR JANUSZ**   **(206) 443-0793**
(AFTRA, SAG)

Audition workshops and private coaching. Janusz is an actor/instructor with regional theatre, film, television and off-Broadway experience, and was artistic director and founder of Seattle's Triad Ensemble, a small Equity theatre company, 1987-1994. He has been guest instructor at Cornish College for the Arts, Bush School, UW, the Centrum Foundation in Port Townsend and the International AIDS Conference in Amsterdam.

■ **MARK JENKINS**   **(206) 323-7499**
(EQUITY, SAG, AFTRA)

Actor/director/teacher Jenkins has been acting for 25 years, on Broadway and off-Broadway in New York, and in television, film and theatre in Los Angeles, Baltimore, San Diego and Seattle. Locally, he has appeared at the Seattle Rep, Intiman, Empty Space and ACT. He is a member of the Actors Studio and a founder of Freehold. He has been teaching for seven years, and currently teaches at Freehold and the University of Washington.

■ **BETTY KOPIT**   **(206) 745-5113**
(EQUITY)

Physical/vocal training; voice work, scene work, and audition and improv techniques. Kopit has taught acting at colleges in New York, Michigan and Colorado, and has been an Artist-in-Residence in Washington and several other states. She is currently teaching at three colleges in the Northwest. She is now in her 16th year of touring her one-woman show.

2.1 Acting Coaches/Stage

■ **GEORGE LEWIS**   **(206) 323-7499**

Private coaching, workshops and movement coaching for plays. An actor/director/teacher, Lewis has been working in movement theatre since 1971. He studied corporeal mime in Paris with Etienne Decroux, circus skills at the French National Circus School and topeng (masked) dance in Bali. He ran his own school in Boston, and has been teaching acting, corporeal mime and movement for actors since 1978, as well as teaching in colleges and universities across the U.S. and Canada. He is currently a member of Freehold.

■ **MICHAEL J. LOGGINS**   **(206) 975-3578**
(Equity, SAG, AFTRA)

Michael J. Loggins has been a teacher and professional actor for over 20 years. A graduate of the London Academy of Dramatic Art, he has taught at many high schools in the area as well as Seattle Children's Theatre. Loggins teaches acting, including vocal and specizalized movement technique, stage combat scene study and performance, dialect coaching, improvisation and cold reading for stage and camera.

■ **CATHERINE MADDEN**   **(206) 368-8544**

Acting and the Alexander Technique; workshops and private coaching that combine stage work and movement theory. Madden is a former Artistic Director of a Midwest theatre company who's taught Alexander Technique for 11 years, and is currently the Alexander instructor in the UW's Professional Acting Program. (See 2.6 Specialty Instruction.)

2.1 Acting Coaches/Stage

■ **JESSICA MARLOWE-GOLDSTEIN   (206) 323-7499**
(EQUITY)

A director, actor and teacher, Marlowe-Goldstein has taught drama in Kathmandu, Nepal, in the New York City Public School system (in Harlem) for seven years and for the Pacific Rim Camp for the Arts. She received her training at the UW's PATP, and teaches acting, Shakespeare and audition technique. At Freehold, Jessica teaches a drop-in audition clinic, and privately coaches individuals in conservatory audition preparation, including monologue selection.

■ **JACKIE MOSCOU**   **(206) 325-9456**
(**EQUITY**)

Special coaching for auditions and stage roles. Moscou attended New York's American Academy of Dramatic Arts and has extensive acting credits at Seattle's leading Equity theatres. Moscou is also a member of SSDC, Society for Stage Directors and Choreographers.

■ **TERRY EDWARD MOORE**   **(206) 789-2689**
(EQUITY, SAG, AFTRA)

Private audition coach; helps actors find clear and specific actions, clarify scansion, etc. Moore has an MFA in Acting/Directing from Brandeis University. He has acted, directed, and taught around the country, including New York, Minneapolis and Phoenix. Terry is one of the founders, and is currently co-artistic director, of Seattle Shakespeare Festival.

2.1 Acting Coaches/Stage

■ **MARJORIE NELSON**   **(206) 329-3097**
(EQUITY, SAG, AFTRA)

Private audition work for the advanced and professional theatre performer. Nelson has appeared in more than 60 of Seattle Rep's productions, as well as other local and regional theatres. She is a certified Alexander Technique teacher.

■ **TAWNYA PETTIFORD-WATES**   **(206) 723-7099**
(EQUITY, SAG, AFTRA)

Individual acting and audition coaching. Tawnya Pettiford-Wates has acted from Broadway to Seattle, and has numerous directing credits from most of the major theatres: Pioneer Square, ACT, S.C.T. and New City. Tawnya, who holds an MFA & a Ph.D. in acting/directing, is head of theatre arts at Seattle Central Community College, and teaches Stage Combat.

■ **HAL RYDER**   **(206) 718-2453**

Private coaching and workshops. Ryder has taught classical acting since 1982, is a member of the Cornish drama faculty, and is artistic director of Open Door Theatre. His workshops, covering classical scene work, stage combat, voice and auditioning techniques, are available periodically.

■ **LARRY SILVERBERG**   **(206) 728-7609**
(EQUITY, SAG)

Private coaching and workshops. Silverberg is a graduate of the Neighborhood Playhouse in New York, where he studied with Sanford Meisner. Since 1986, he has been teaching professional classes in Meisner work while continuing his acting career in feature films, television, off-Broadway and regional theatre. A director and award-winning film-maker, Silverberg has written two books, *The Sanford Meisner Approach: An Actor's Workbook*, and *Loving to Audition an Actor's Workbook*. He is artistic director of the Belltown Theatre Centre.

■ **ROBIN LYNN SMITH**   **(206) 323-7499**
(EQUITY, SAG, AFTRA)

A professional director and teacher, Smith has worked in Chicago, Boston and New York. Since moving to Seattle from New York six years ago, she has directed at the Seattle Rep, Empty Space, Seattle Children's Theatre and New City. She has been a guest director/faculty member at New York University, University of Washington and Cornish College for the Arts. She holds an MFA in Directing from NYU and a BFA in Acting from Boston University. Smith is now a member of Freehold.

■ **JAYNE TAINI**   **(206) 324-2458**
(EQUITY, SAG, AFTRA)

Ongoing scene study workshop on Monday nights; by audition only. Taini has extensive stage, film and TV experience, and has appeared at most of Seattle's major theatres. She has taught acting for 14 years. Also available for private coaching.

■ **JIM TAYLOR**   **(206) 323-1288**
(AFTRA)

Trained at the Actor's Studio and Second City, Jim Taylor is an actor/director/teacher who has appeared off-Broadway and in Manhattan clubs. Bringing 33 years of teaching experience to his coaching, he can "assist in making choices that will make actors confident in auditions."

2.1 Acting Coaches/Stage

■ JOHN VREEKE   (206) 937-8872

Vreeke is primarily a regional theatre director with 20 years' experience directing and teaching on all levels, community, university and professional, including seven years with the Alley Theatre in Houston, associate director of the Arkansas Repertory Theatre in Little Rock, Arkansas and locally with Alice B. and Book-It. Most recently, he was associate producer for the television series "Northern Exposure" where he was heavily involved with casting. In addition to private audition coaching, basic acting skills, Shakespeare and script analysis, he teaches a six-person workshop focusing on the similarities and differences between acting for stage and acting for camera.

■ LAUREL ANNE WHITE   (206) 784-3464
(EQUITY, AFTRA)

Acting and audition coach who incorporates personalized voice and body work. Helps new-to-intermediate level performers choose and refine audition material. White is an actor/director with extensive experience in major regional theatres, and camera credits including "Twin Peaks" and "Northern Exposure." She holds an MFA from the U.W. PATP, has taught at the U.W, Evergreen State, SCT and Village.

Portland

■ BARBARA KITE (503) 287-1093

Barbara Kite is a working New York trained actress, director and acting coach. She graduated from the American Academy of Dramatic Arts in NYC, where she won its Jellinger award for acting. Available for private coaching in addition to classes, she specializes in teaching students seeking a professional career, as well as professionals seeking to grow in their art.

Custom Monologues

■ **PAMELA SACKETT**   **(206) 632-0059**

Sackett is a noted Seattle playwright who specializes in creating custom monologues for the professional actor and actor-in-training through private consultations and workshops. Sackett also specializes in writing plays for special populations. She is the author of *Two Minutes to Shine: Thirty Potent New Monologues for the Auditioning Actor* and *Two Minutes to Shine, Book Two and Book Three* (published by Samuel French, Inc., New York; $8.95).

■ **TONI DOUGLASS**   **(206) 244-7558**

(See above for custom monologues.)

STUDIOS

Seattle

■ **BELLTOWN THEATRE CENTER**
115 Blanchard
Seattle, WA 98121
(206) 781-6648

Contact: Larry Silverberg, Artistic Director. BTC offers the Meisner training, recognized by Sanford Meisner in the Northwest. The class meets twice weekly (Monday evenings and Saturday mornings) for six months, and is taught by Larry Silverberg.

■ **FREEHOLD**
1525 - 10th Ave.
Seattle, WA 98122
(206) 323-7499

Originally founded in 1986 as Pasqualini-Smith Studio, Freehold was established in 1991 as a "collaboration of theatre artists committed to deepening the transformational power of theatre through education, experimentation and performance." Freehold offers both acting training and a laboratory theatre for in-house productions.

Serving over 1,000 adult students per year, classes range from beginning acting for the general public to master classes and workshops for working professionals. A representative list of classes is: Basic & Advanced Core Progression in Acting, Voice, Dance & Singing for Actors, Stage Combat, The Actor's Presence, Commercial Acting, Directors Lab, Verse/ Shakespeare, Audition, Suzuki Training Workshop, Playwriting, Getting Started and Alexander Technique. Various summer intensives are offered around a specific topic such as Shakespeare, Chekhov or Improvisation. There are four 10- to12-week

2.2 Studios

terms per year—fall, winter, spring and summer—with daytime, evening and weekend classes. The public is invited to open houses before every term, to meet the teachers.

Located in the historic Oddfellows Hall in the Pike/ Pine corridor on the border of Capitol Hill and First Hill, Freehold has four studio spaces for classes and a 99-seat performance facility for developmental works and new experimental approaches to old plays.

The staff are all working professionals, including Robin Lynn Smith, Mark Jenkins, George Lewis, Richard Brestoff, Althea Hukari, James Lapan, Jessica Marlow-Goldstein, Cathy Madden, Timothy Piggee, Suzie Schneider and Matt Smith. (See 2.2 Coaches, this chapter.)

■ THE GREENWOOD STUDIO
8312 Greenwood Ave. N
Seattle, WA 98103
(206) 783-9156

Contact: Molly Anderson. The Greenwood Studio offers classes in Beginning to Advanced Acting, Singing & Vocal Production, Stage Combat and Speaking Voice, as well as workshops in Musical Comedy and Improvisation. The staff are all working professionals.

PERFORMANCE WORKSHOPS
PRIVATE TUTORIALS

ACTING • AUDITIONING • DIALECTS • IMPROV

MOVEMENT • MUSICAL THEATRE • STAGE COMBAT

SINGING • VOICE & SPEECH

Special guest artist - Gary Austin of L.A. - teaches Improvisation

Studio Stage & Performance Hall - available for rental.

8312 Greenwood Ave N, Seattle, WA 98103

206.783.9156 • 206.783.9183

■ NORTHWEST ACTORS STUDIO
1100 East Pike
Seattle, WA 98122
(206) 324-6328
Fax: (206) 860-1932

Founded in 1977, the Studio offers a complete acting curriculum year-round for youth and adults, from the beginner through the professional level. In addition to basic craft classes, the Studio offers Improvisation, Musical Theatre, Comedy, Playwrighting, Voice, Shakespeare, Audition Technique, an ongoing Scene Study Workshop for working professionals and a two-year conservatory program. Director and co-founder Ann Graham is joined by a staff of working Seattle actors. Registration is ongoing; sessions begin in January, April, July, and September. Call for a brochure. Capitol Hill.

■ STUDIO EAST
402 - 6th St. S
Kirkland, WA 98033
(206) 827-3123

Contact: Lani Brockman. Studio East provides year-round training to youth and adults, beginning through professionals in all levels and aspects of theatre. Curriculum includes Acting Technique, Audition, Shakespeare, Improvisation, Stage Combat, Musical Theatre, Dance, Commercial Acting, Stage Management and more. From September through June, Studio East also offers a home-school program and daily pre-school classes. All teachers are working professionals with extensive teaching experience.

Five to six production classes are mounted each year with youth and adults; they range from one-acts to full-length musicals and are performed in the studio theatre. Studio East also offers a six-week comprehensive Young Actors Professional Intensive in the summer for young adults ages 13 to 20 (entrance by audition only). Also

2.2 Studios

offered in the summer are two-week theatre camps for ages 8 to15.

■ **THE WESTLAKE ACTOR'S STUDIO**
1219 Westlake
Seattle, WA 98109
(206) 284-5720

Contact: Richard Brestoff & Kimberly White. Seattle's newest studio is a merger of Kimberly White's Studio and the Camera Smart Actor's Lab. Brestoff teaches classes dedicated to equipping actors with the techniques needed to do their best in front of the camera. Classes are offered for all levels of ability and include: Personalization and the Camera, Craft and the Camera, Character and the Camera. Taught by veteran Hollywood actor Richard Brestoff, the on-camera classes teach many aspects not only of acting for the camera; but general understanding of the filming process and set etiquette. (See 2.3 Commercial Training.) Kimberly White, a certified Linklater voice teacher, teaches the speaking voice and Shakespeare. Alexander Technique is also offered.

■ **WEST SEATTLE THEATRE ARTS**
10015 - 28th St. SW
Seattle, WA 98146
(206) 935-9782

Contact: Cate Koler. A year-round theatre educational program for children and adults of all levels of experience. Located in West Seattle, it offers a wide variety of specialty classes, including: Beginning Acting, Creative Dramatics, Musical Theatre, and Physical Comedy Theatre. For the committed young actor, a year-long company class combines all of the above as well as camera acting, Shakespeare and other specialty topics (payment for this class is on a monthly basis). West Seattle Theatre Arts operates out of two different locations in West Seattle, primarily at West Side School. Opportunities to

perform are through the affiliated company, KidsTheatre.
(See 4.3 Workshops & Youth Theatre.)

Portland

■ **PORTLAND ACTOR'S CONSERVATORY**
Firehouse Theatre
1436 SW Montgomery
Portland, OR 97201
(503) 274-1717
Fax: (503) 274-0511

Contact: Beth Harper. Formerly Training Ground
Actor's Studio. Founded in 1985. the Portland Actors'
Conservatory has a two-year full-time conservatory
program, as well as an academy program for part-time
students. Classes in stage and camera acting are taught
by working professionals. The curriculum embraces an
eclectic approach to method and technique, and focuses
on training the complete actor. Fees are $50-$240; private
coaching is $30 per hour.

COMMERCIAL TRAINING

September

Seattle

■ **DENNIS BATEMAN**   **(206) 689-6227**
(EQUITY, SAG, AFTRA)

Voice-over coaching and demo tape production offered to individuals and small groups. Bateman is a professional voice talent, former head of voice-overs at the New York AFTRA A/V Center, and has done commercials, industrials and talking books. His classes stress copy analysis, mic technique, interpretation, character, and how to get the job. Wedgewood.

■ **BELLEVUE COMMUNITY COLLEGE**
                                    (206) 641-2263

BCC offers various 10-week classes, including In Front of the Camera, and Radio and TV Commercials. The enrollment is limited; classes are taught in fall, winter and spring quarters through the continuing education program by Pat French. (See below).

■ **RICHARD BRESTOFF**   **(206) 284-5720**

Richard Brestoff, proprietor of the Westlake Actor's Studio, is also available for private coaching. Brestoff holds an M.F.A. in Acting from New York University, where his teachers included master teacher Peter Kass, Olympia Dukakis, Kristen Linklater and Joe Chaikin. He is a three-time prime time Emmy awards judge, and appeared on the Emmy ballot himself for an episode of *thirtysomething*. He has acted in over a dozen feature films and over 30 network television shows, has taught at the UW, Freehold, and Seattle Central Community college and

2.3 Commercial Training

has written two books on acting: *The Camera Smart Actor* and *The Great Acting Teachers and their Methods*. His teaching is based on the principles of Stanislavsky Vakhtangov and others, but is not rooted in the "method." (See 2.2 Studios, The Camera Smart Studio.)

■ **PAT FRENCH** (206) 746-7606

Commercial acting workshops. French, an experienced voice actor and radio drama director, and Bellevue Community College's commercial acting instructor for the past 20 years, offers classes on Saturdays: Acting in Front of the Camera, 9:00 a.m.-12:30 p.m. (limited to 10 students) and Radio/TV Commercials, 1:00 p.m.-4:30 p.m.. In addition, Pat teaches Cold Readings and Advanced Acting. Bellevue.

■ **PHIL HARPER** (206) 282-5368
(AFTRA, SAG)

Commercial voice consultant; Harper is one of the Northwest's leading commercial voice talents, and offers informal phone consultations to commercial actors who are either new to this market or new to voice work.

■ **KALLES-LEVINE PRODUCTIONS** (206) 447-9318

Commercial acting and film acting workshops. Classes include: Quick-Start Commercial Audition Workshop (one evening, $40), Weekend Intensive for Commercial Acting (two days, $200); an on-camera class (enrollment limited); Advanced Commercial Television Class (follow-up to weekend class, $75); Kid Class ($65 for children 5 to 12); and Film and Monologue Study for Teens and Adults ($75). Classes are taught by casting directors Patti Kalles and Laurie Levine. Downtown Seattle.

2.3 Commercial Training

■ JODI ROTHFIELD CASTING ASSOCIATES, CSA
(206) 448-0927

Offers both beginning and advanced commercial/film workshops for the serious, professional actor. Introductory class addresses the business side of being an actor and on-camera training. Advanced classes are for experienced actors. Adult classes are taught by Jodi Rothfield. Kids' and teens' classes are also offered, taught by Cate Macapia. Enrollment is limited and a deposit is required.

■ HEIDI WALKER   **(206) 622-9646**

On-camera acting and confidence-building workshops to develop camera acting skills and audition technique. Heidi Walker has worked in casting for 13 years, both in L.A. and in Seattle.

■ VERONICA WEIKEL   **(206) 547-3230**
(AFTRA)

Commercial voice teacher; offers private instruction in TV/radio voice-over, audition and cold reading techniques. Also, a voice-over intensive (four students maximum). Weikel, whose voice workshops come recommended by Seattle's leading talent agents, is a working professional with over 20 years in commercial voice work. Wallingford.

■ THE WESTLAKE ACTOR'S STUDIO
(206) 284-5720
(See 2.2 Studios.)

2.3 Commercial Training

Portland

■ **BARBARA BALSZ**   **(503) 245-6343**

Film and commercial acting classes, including on-camera work, audition techniques and cold readings. Balsz has taught acting and audition techniques for the camera for over 18 years.

■ **NURMI HUSA**   **(360) 694-3641**
(EQUITY, SAG, AFTRA)

Voice demo coach; Husa is a well-known Portland actor/director who works with new voice-over talent to develop their first tape, as well as experienced commercial actors to develop new performance levels. Two sessions, plus on-site assistance at the recording studio. Private coaching available, as well as dialect coaching for stage or commercial work.

■ **PETE RANDALL**   **(503) 292-5610**
(AFTRA, SAG)

Commercial voice coach; by interview only. Separate weekly workshops for the committed beginner and the experienced voice-over actor. Limited enrollment. Randall is a well-known commercial/corporate voice actor in Portland.

SPEAKING VOICE & DIALECTS

Seattle

■ **DEENA BURKE**   (206) 789-8294
(Equity)

Voice, speech, and dialect coach. Deena is an actor with extensive graduate and undergraduate teaching experience. Although she teaches Skinner speech and bases her work on the Berry technique, she nevertheless combines many approaches to allow the actor's creative impulses to be released through the voice. Deena, a Juilliard graduate, is the first-year voice and speech teacher in the Conservatory Acting Program at Cornish College of the Arts and has coached at most of the major theatres in town.

■ **STEVIE KALLOS**   (206) 367-3087

With 20 years' experience as an actor under her belt and an M.F.A. from the UW's PATP, Kallos has coached voice and dialects at most of the major theatres in the area. Currently she is on the faculty at Cornish and Freehold. Her philosophy is that "all vocal and speech 'techniques' must serve and deepen acting values." Areas of expertise include: dialects, accent reduction, audition coaching, Shakespeare, text.

■ **KATHRYN MESNEY**   (206) 567-4761
(Equity, SAG, AFTRA)

Actor/voice coach; specializes in British, European, and American dialects & Lessac Vocal Technique. Mesney has taught voice and dialects for 18 years, and heads the voice/speech program in the Conservatory Acting Program at Cornish College of the Arts.

■ **JUDITH SHAHN**   **(206) 286-1854**
(Equity, SAG, AFTRA)

Voice/dialect coach. Designated Linklater voice teacher (certified by Kristin Linklater, July 1991). Voice/dialect teacher for University of Washington's Professional Actor Training Program (PATP), as well as vocal coach for the Oregon Shakespeare Festival in Ashland and at most of Seattle's theatres. Shahn specializes in voice production for the actor: freeing the voice, increasing range and power, and Shakespearean text. Dialects: British Isles (including various Irish, Scottish, and Northern English), European, and most American.

■ **ELLEN TAFT, ADVS**   **(206) 323-6983**

Voice/speech/dialects teacher and vocal coach for Pilgrim Center for the Arts, Taft received the Advanced Diploma of Voice Studies from London's Central School of Speech and Drama in 1989, where she attended workshops with Cicely Berry. In addition, she has taken workshops with Kristen Linklater and Arthur Lessac. Taft works on breathing, relaxation, alignment and projection, dialects and text work, especially Shakespeare. Taft bases her teaching on the principles of anatomy, physiology, and acoustics, as well as the psycho-physiological connection between thought and spontaneous vocal production. Her approach is very physical and incorporates Tai Chi, Alexander Technique, Yoga—and, indeed, even cheerleading at times.

An experienced teacher of ESL and German, she also works with foreign-born actors seeking to acquire a more American accent, and coaches opera singers in German diction and phrasing. A former resident of the U.K.,

(London, Yorkshire and the West Country) she teaches British (RP and provincial dialects), American regional and foreign accents. Taft is the former artistic director of Philadelphia's Shakespeare in the Park, and teaches classes in *Shakespeare and the Actor's Voice*, using Shakespearean texts to develop and free the natural voice.

■ **VOICETECH** (206) 448-0787

A unique comprehensive training center for the speaking and singing voice. Karen Oleson works on voice development: range, resonance projection, accent reduction. Voicetech is a place to "learn how to use your everyday voice in a healthy way."

■ **KIMBERLY WHITE** (206) 284-5720

A graduate of Cal Arts, Kimberly White was certified by Kristen Linklater in 1993 and has been on the faculty of Shakespeare and Co. in Lennox, Connecticut, at the UW's PATP and Freehold. White bases her teaching on freeing and strengthening the natural voice, releasing creative impulses, and enhancing the connection between the actor's inner life and the voice. She teaches privately and through her studio, Westlake Actor's Center.

Portland

■ **CAREN GRAHAM** (503) 282-2691

Graham holds an M.F.A. from the University of Washington's PATP and has attended Linklater workshops, although she draws on the techniques of Lessac and Berry as well. Although based in Portland, she taught for four years at Cornish College of the Arts, and at several Shakespeare Festivals, including the Oregon Shakespeare Festival, Portland. She has taught several arts-in-the-schools workshops and Shakespeare for young actors.

■ **NURMI HUSA**
Vancouver, WA
(360) 694-3641

Nurmi Husa, a voice talent, also teaches dialects. (See 2.3 Commercial Training.)

Alaska

■ **TOM SKORE**   **(907) 786-1740**
(Equity, AFTRA)

Skore offers private coaching in speech technique, primarily grounded in Linklater and Lessac: elimination of regionalisms, dialect training, acting and audition technique. He is an actor/director with 15 years' teaching experience at graduate and undergraduate levels: Ohio University, Southern Oregon State College and currently, the University of Alaska, Anchorage.

SINGING TEACHERS & MUSICAL AUDITION COACHES

Seattle

■ **EMILIE BERNE** **(206) 784-8008**

Voice instruction, and song styling techniques for jazz, musical theatre & cabaret audition, as well as performance. Berne is a pianist, composer-arranger, voice teacher and music director with over 25 years of professional experience in Seattle and San Francisco. Her students perform regionally and internationally on main stages and cruise ships, in national touring companies and cabarets. Career guidance, practice tapes and resource library are available. Beginners to professional. Ballard.

■ **JEFF CALDWELL** **(206) 328-2106**

Jeff Caldwell has extensive experience training classical and musical theatre singers. For six years he taught at UW's PATP, and currently teaches at Freehold. Caldwell has been music director for ACT, Group Theatre, Cabaret de Paris and Civic Light Opera. Capitol Hill.

■ **BARBARA COFFIN** **(206) 324-7002**
(SAG, AFTRA, Equity)

The fundamentals of singing, vocal technique and performance coaching. Beginners to advanced. Private lessons and with the UW's Experimental College. A veteran Seattle performer, Coffin has performed at the Fifth Avenue Musical Theatre, many opera companies, on cruise ships and in nightclubs. Capitol Hill.

■ **PAUL GATES** (206)720-0651

Gates is a singing teacher working on basic vocal technique, breathing and focus. Gates is an experienced choral conductor, soloist and recitalist, and has sung with the Seattle Opera. Judkins.

■ **BRIAN HIGHAM** (206) 322-0948
(Equity, SAG, AFTRA)

Audition coaching and voice instruction. Higham is an actor/singer, and is an active musical director in the Seattle area. He has taught singing for 16 years. Mt. Baker.

■ **MARY LEVINE** (206) 283-5553

Musical theatre audition coach. Levine is a veteran vocal coach, working in musical theatre, opera and concert, who has performed in over 200 musicals in the U.S. and Canada. She is listed in the *Who's Who* music directory. Levine is former musical director for the Civic Light Opera, and tour pianist for Seattle Opera's school shows and American Ballet Theatre (NYC) International tours. Magnolia.

■ **ELLEN MCLAIN** (206)282-1531
(Equity, AFTRA, SAG, AGMA)

Voice teacher and audition coach, McLain has an M.M. from the New England Conservatory of Music in Boston. A veteran of 24 years, she has performed on Broadway, throughout the country and in Europe, in both musical theatre and opera. Queen Anne.

2.5 Singing

■ **TERESA METZGER**   **(206) 937-6565**

Audition prep for musical theatre. Metzger is an experienced music director with credits at The Bathhouse, The Seattle Group Theatre, Tacoma Actors Guild and Seattle Children's Theatre. West Seattle.

■ **JULIE MIREL**   **(206) 323-6238**
(Equity AGMA)

Singer, teacher, and audition and musical theatre coach. Mirel has 30 years' professional experience, and has performed many principal roles with Seattle Opera, Seattle Symphony, and numerous western regional companies. Madrona.

■ **JOHANNA MOLLOY**   **(206) 823-8284**

Singing and performance technique. Molloy uses a variety of methods to free the natural voice and encourage the joy of singing. She has studied on scholarship at USC, with Lee Strasberg, Marni Nixon and Herta Glatz, and has sung professionally for over 20 years. Workshops available. Kirkland.

■ **KAREN OLESON**   **(206) 448-0787**

A singing teacher, with over 20 years' experience in vocal technique, Karen also coaches musical theatre. (See Voicetech.)

■ **VOICETECH**   **(206) 448-0787**

A unique comprehensive training center for the speaking and singing voice. Seattle singer/instructor Karen Oleson heads up the studio, whose guest instructors include commercial voice talents, professional singers and certified voice therapists. Karen holds an M.A. in vocal performance, and has over 20 years' experience as a teacher. Workshops range from four to six weeks.

2.5 Singing

■ **PENELOPE VRACHOPOULOS**   **(206) 454-1906**

Voice and interpretation for actors and singers. Vrachopoulos, an actor/singer and director, has a Ph.D. in Music from Stanford University and has been teaching singing for 28 years. She is also Artistic Director of Bellevue Opera, a project of The Peccadillo Players.

■ **MARIANNE WELTMANN**   **(206) 524-5195**

Singing coach. Weltmann has an M.A. from The Juilliard School, and performs in New York and Europe. Her students include working professionals in opera, theatre and concert locally and nationwide. She specializes in breathing and alignment, and is certified in massage therapy. She has taught singing for over 20 years. Ravenna.

■ **ANN EVANS ZAVADA**   **(206) 440-0084**

Private lessons, vocal technique and application, beginners to advanced. Zavada specializes in producing healthy "Broadway Belt." She has performed locally at Fifth Avenue Theatre and extensively in summer stock. North End.

SPECIALTY INSTRUCTION

<u>Alexander Technique</u>

Seattle

■ **LYNNE COMPTON**   (206) 623-8588 ext. 2

Group Class or private coaching. Compton is a member of Alexander Technique International and is a licensed massage therapist.

■ **CATHERINE KETTRICK**   (206) 522-3584

Group classes/private coaching. Kettrick belongs to Alexander Technique International, and has taught since 1976.

■ **CATHERINE MADDEN**   (206) 368-8544

(See 2.1 Coaches.)

■ **RICHARD MARENS**   (206) 781-1804

Private coaching. Marens is a graduate of the Alexander Training Institute.

■ **MARJORIE NELSON**   (206) 329-3097

Private lessons. Nelson is certified by both the American and British societies of Alexander Technique.

■ **ANDREW ZAVADA**   (206) 440-0084

Private lessons. Zavada is a graduate of the American Center for the Alexander Technique in New York. He is certified by and a member of NASTAT (North American Society of Teachers of the Alexander Technique). House calls.

2.6 Specialty Instruction

Tacoma

■ **JANE CARR**   **(206) 759-0696**

Group classes, private lessons, and lecture
demonstrations. Jane Carr is certified by NASTAT (North
American Society of Teachers of the Alexander
Technique.)

■ **JOHN CARR**   **(206) 759-0696**

Group classes and private lessons. John Carr has an
undergraduate degree from Goodman School of Drama,
and is certified by NASTAT.

Feldenkrais Method

■ **JUDITH MARCUS**   **(206) 547-7002**

Private sessions. Marcus is a member of Feldenkrais
Guild. She specializes in somatic psychology.

■ **JILEEN RUSSELL**   **(206) 937-5493, (206) 932-2919**

Group classes in ATM (Awareness Through
Movement), and individuals lessons. Russell is certified
by the Guild of Feldenkrais Practitioners.

2.6 Specialty Instruction

Fencing

■ **LEONID BENCEL**   **(206) 282-5479**

Classic stage fencing and saber instruction. Bencel has been a fencing instructor for more than 20 years, and is the founder of one of Seattle's leading fencing associations.

Improvisation

■ **BRUCE BAKER**   **(206) 526-1540**

Improv for all skill levels. Baker works with small groups and individuals, and has taught improv since 1980. He is the founder of Playful U: the Improvisational Acting Center, "Wheel of Improv," the "Theatre on the Spot" television show and the "Do-it-Yourself Video Show."

■ **EDWARD SAMPSON**   **(206) 842-5181**
(EQUITY, AFTRA)

Sampson has been a Seattle stage actor for 15 years. In collaboration with Matt Smith as Stark Raving Theatre, he has created many award-winning shows: *Here & There*, *Kitty*, *Last Supper* and *Little Men on the Feminine Landscape*. Sampson holds workshops several times a year.

■ **MATT SMITH**   **(206) 323-2878**
(AFTRA, SAG)

Smith offers private classes for beginning and advanced students, as well as a month-long workshop at Freehold (usually in August and February.) He is a solo performer and Co-Artistic Director of Stark Raving Theatre.

■ **UNEXPECTED PRODUCTIONS**   **(206) 587-2414**

Eight-week improv workshops.

2.6 Specialty Instruction

<u>Mime</u>

■ **GEORGE LEWIS**
(206) 323-7499

> (See 2.1 Coaches.)

<u>Movement Therapy</u>

■ **CENTER FOR MOVEMENT ARTS & THERAPY**
(206) 547-8034

> Contact: Margaret Sutro, co-director.

■ **INSTITUTE FOR TRANSFORMATIONAL**
MOVEMENT
916 NE 65th St. #158
Seattle, WA 98115
(206) 523-3286

> Contact: Joyce Izumi. Performance-oriented movement and movement therapy. Individual sessions and workshops.

<u>Stage Combat</u>

■ **GEOFFREY ALM**   **(206) 323-7499**

Specializes in rapier and dagger, broadsword, smallsword, quarterstaff and unarmed combat. Alm is an actor/fight choreographer, a certified teacher and a member of The Society of American Fight Directors. He also teaches certification and re-certification classes at Freehold.

■ **ROBERT MACDOUGALL**   **(206) 522-2201**

MacDougall is a stage combat specialist (armed and unarmed techniques): Fight Director with the Society of American Fight Directors, Fight Master with Society of Australian Fight Directors, member of the United

Stuntman's Association and certified in several martial arts. In addition, he is a certified Feldenkrais practitioner and licensed massage therapist. He also offers general coaching in movement, with private and group sessions available. A movement teacher at Cornish College of the Arts, MacDougall teaches Tai Chi and Yoga, as well.

■ **TAWNYA PETTIFORD-WATES**   **(206) 723-7099**

Stage fight specialist, actor/choreographer, and member of both the American and British Fight Director Societies. Her specialty is unarmed combat.

Movement

■ **ROBERT DAVIDSON**   **(206) 324-6221**

Davidson, a dancer, teacher and choreographer, teaches low-flying trapeze and Skinner Releasing Technique weekly in the University District. Davidson is currently on the PATP movement faculty in the UW School of Drama, and is director of his own performing company.

■ **DAVID TAFT**   **(206) 368-3514**
(Equity, AFTRA)

Private classes in movement, specializing in the neutral, expressive and Commedia dell' Arte masks. David Taft teaches movement, bio-mechanics and Commedia dell'Arte at Cornish College of the Arts.

■ **ROBERT MACDOUGALL**   **(206) 522-2201**

(See Stage Combat, above.)

DANCE STUDIOS

Seattle

■ **AMERICAN DANCE INSTITUTE**
8001 Greenwood Ave. N
Seattle, WA 98103
(206) 783-0755

Contact: Elizabeth Chayer, director. All levels: ballet, flamenco, ballroom and tap. For the very young, ADI offers Creative Dance and parent/toddler classes Live/recorded music, no showers. Greenwood. Metro buses 5, 48.

■ **BALLET ACADEMY OF PERFORMING ARTS**
22811 - 100th Ave. W
Edmonds, WA 98020
(206) 771-4525

Ballet, jazz, and tap at all levels for ages three to adult. Classes are month-to-month in brand-new studios. Recorded music, no showers.

■ **THE BALLET STUDIO**
4556 University Way NE
Seattle, WA 98105
(206) 329-9166

Contact: Maren Erickson. Ballet for adults, six days a week; generally afternoons and early evening, but also Thursday and Saturday mornings. Registration is exclusively through the Experimental College for the entire term; no class cards available. Live musical accompaniment, no showers. Accessible by bus. U-District.

2.7 Dance Studios

■ **THE BBC STUDIO**
2211 First Ave.
Seattle, WA 98121
(206) 441-6071.

Offers ballet, flamenco, Yoga, Tai Chi, Kung Fu, belly dancing and conditioning classes. Belltown. Metro buses 2, 4, 16, 17, 18, 21.

■ **CAMEO DANCE–GREENLAKE**
7220 Woodlawn Ave. NE
Seattle, WA 98115
(206) 528-8183

Classes and workshops for adults and children in tap, ballet, jazz and gymnastics; live music, no showers. Greenlake. Metro buses 16, 48.

■ **CENTER FOR DANCE**
485 Front St. N
Issaquah, WA 98027
(206) 391-5060

Beginning to advanced ballet, jazz, modern, musical theatre and tap for children and adults. Registration is by the session. Recorded music accompaniment. Showers. Metro routes 210, 211, 274. Eastside.

■ **CORNISH COLLEGE OF THE ARTS**
710 E Roy
Seattle, WA 98102
(206) 323-1400 ext. 3019

Beginning classes in ballet and modern dance two evenings a week, September through May. Saturday classes for children. Also a summer program in modern, jazz and ballet. Live music, showers. Capitol Hill. Metro bus 7.

2.7 Dance Studios

■ CREATIVE DANCE CENTER
12577 Densmore Ave. N
Seattle, WA 98133
(206) 363-7281

A studio for children, located in the Haller Lake
Community Club, with classes in creative dance, folk and
jazz. Both live and recorded music. Drop-in classes or by
the term. Haller Lake.

■ DANCE ON! CAPITOL HILL
340 - 15th Ave. E
Seattle, WA 98112
(206) 325-6697
Fax: (206) 325-2087

Morning and evening classes in ballet, modern, jazz,
tap, Afro-Cuban and exercise; independent instructors in
belly dancing and yoga. Children, adults and seniors,
beginner through professional. Rehearsal/performance
spaces available for rental. Artistic Director, Shirley
Jenkins. Capitol Hill.

■ ELIZABETH'S DANCE DIMENSIONS
12121 NE Northrup Way
Bellevue, WA 98005
(206) 883-2206

Ballet, tap, hip-hop, lyrical and jazz classes for
children and adults from beginning to professional levels.
Classes on drop-in or month-to month basis. Eastside.

■ EMILY'S DANCE ARTS
547 - 156th Ave. SE
Bellevue, WA 98007
(206) 746-3659

Ballet, tap, jazz, modern and hip-hop for all levels
and ages. Recorded music. Eastside.

■ **EWAJO CENTER, INC.**
2719 E Madison
Seattle, WA 98112
(206) 322-0155

Afro, Latin, jazz, iso-rhythmics, ballet and modern for children, adults and seniors. Music is mostly recorded. Classes are drop-in or by the quarter. No showers. Madison Valley.

■ **JOHNSON & PETERS TAP DANCE STUDIO**
6600 First Ave. NE
Seattle, WA 98115
(206) 729-7620

Contact: Cheryl Johnson and Anthony Peters. Seattle's tap dancing duo specializes in rhythm tap for the serious student. Afternoon, evening and Saturday classes for adults and children ages seven and up. Recorded music, showers. Greenlake.

■ **KATHY'S STUDIO OF DANCE**
4210 SW Edmunds St.
Seattle, WA 98116
(206) 935-3777

Beginning to advanced ballet, tap, jazz acrobatics and hip-hop for ages three through adult. Recorded music. West Seattle.

■ **MARTHA NISHITANI MODERN DANCE**
4205 University Way, NE
Seattle, WA 98105
(206) 633-2456

Late-afternoon and evening classes in modern, ballet and jazz; children's creative dance on Saturdays. Rehearsal space. U-District.

2.7 Dance Studios

■ OLYMPIC BALLET
700 Main St.
Edmonds, WA 98020
(206) 774-7570

Contact: John or Helen Wilkens. Ballet school and semi-professional performing company. Classes in ballet and jazz for all ages and levels. Produces up to 15 full-length performances each year. Tech work and performance opportunities for dancers and occasionally actors. Live music, showers. Edmonds.

■ PACIFIC NORTHWEST BALLET
301 Mercer St.	1660 124th NE
Seattle, WA 98109	Bellevue, WA 98005
(206) 441-9411	(206) 451-1241

Morning and evening classes in ballet; evening sessions available for jazz. Classes are $9 each. Affiliated with the Pacific Northwest Ballet Company. Live music, showers and full dressing rooms. Seattle PNB is at Seattle Center, with many bus connections.

■ RAINER DANCE CENTER
9264 - 57th Ave. S
Seattle, WA 98118
(206) 721-3133

Ballet, tap, jazz and gymnastics for ages preschool to adult, all levels. Classes are month-to-month or drop-in. Recorded music. Metro bus 7. Rainier Valley.

2.7 Dance Studios

■ **SEATTLE CONTEMPORARY BALLET CENTER**
915 E Pine #300
Seattle, WA 98122
(206) 726-1566

Roy Hodgson, a dancer with professional credits off-Broadway, emphasizes anatomical correctness and strengthening in modern, jazz and ballet. A graduate of Cornish's B.F.A. program, Hodgson also holds an M.A. in Kinesiology. Live and recorded music. Oddfellows building in Capitol Hill. E-mail: scbcdance@aol.com.

■ **SPECTRUM DANCE THEATRE**
800 Lake Washington Blvd.
Seattle, WA 98122
(206) 325-4161

Day and evening classes in jazz, ballet, tap and African; single classes $5 to $7. Children's classes available. Discounts available for seven-week sessions. Rehearsal space available for rental. Live music; no shower. Artistic Director: Dale Merrill. Madrona. Metro bus 2 and ample parking.

■ **VELOCITY**
915 E Pine St., Second Floor
Seattle, WA 98122
(206) 325-8773

Modern, jazz, ballet, karate, funk, West African, tango and tumbling, as well as special workshops, for beginning to advanced students. Live and recorded music. Oddfellows building, Capitol Hill.

2.7 Dance Studios

■ **WA ACADEMY OF PERFORMING ARTS**
10847 NE 68th St.
Redmond, WA 98052
(206) 883-2214

Ballet, jazz, tap, modern and musical theater for kids and adults. Live/recorded music, showers. Redmond.

■ **WESTLAKE DANCE CENTER**
2025 Eighth Ave.
Seattle, WA 98121
(206) 621-7378

Westlake Dance Center specializes in teaching beginning to advanced adult jazz; L.A. style and lyrical. Also musical theatre workshops, turns technique classes and ballet. Classes are on a drop-in basis. Recorded musical accompaniment. Dressing rooms equipped with showers. Downtown Seattle.

3

The
Commercial Actor

TALENT AGENTS

Washington (Union Franchised)

N.B. *The Actor's Handbook* does not recommend paying an agent for expensive photo packages. **For a list of recommended photographers and their going rates, please see 5.2 In a Supporting Role, Photographers** (prices range from $65 to $210).

■ **ACTORS & WALKER AGENCY** (AFTRA)
600 First Ave. #234
Seattle, WA 98104
(206) 68-AGENT/ 682-4368
Fax: (206) 223-1883

Contact: A. Elicia Walker. Actors & Walker is a small agency looking for established and well-trained professionals of all ages with experience. Send picture/resume; no follow-up calls or drop-ins, please.

■ **THE ACTORS GROUP** (AFTRA, SAG)
114 Alaskan Way S #104
Seattle, WA 98104
(206) 624-9465
Fax: (206) 624-9466

Contact: Tish Lopez. The Actors Group represents over 100 performers, mostly seasoned union talent with a stage background. Lopez has several years in the business, and runs a small, energetic agency. Experienced Seattle talent are invited to send photo/resume/voice tape. No follow-up calls, please. The agent will respond if interested.

3.1 Talent Agents

■ **CLASSIC PROMOTIONS INC.** (AFTRA)
1600 Dexter Ave. N #501
Seattle, WA 98109
(206) 285-0961
Fax: (206) 488-7208

Contact: Judy Gratton. Classic Promotions requests copies of headshots and resumes. No follow-up calls, please.

■ **DRAMATIC ARTISTS AGENCY** (AFTRA. SAG)
1000 Lenora # 511
Seattle WA 98121
(206) 442-9190
Fax: (206) 442-9192

Contact: Audra Brown. The Dramatic Artists Agency represents adults and children from age four for work in radio, television, film, industrial, voice-overs, CD-Rom/ Interactive, industrial, trade shows/live performances and commercial print. Send a photo and resume. If interested, the agency will schedule a private audition. No follow-up calls, please.

■ **E. THOMAS BLISS & ASSOCIATES, INC.**
(AFTRA, SAG, AEA, WGA)
219 First Ave. S #420
Seattle, WA 98104
(206) 340-1875
Fax: (206) 340-1194

Contact: Michael and Thomas Bliss. Seattle's most franchised agency represents actors, singers, dancers, voices, stunt players and other show business professionals. Send photos and resumes; no follow-up calls, please.

■ **LOLA HALLOWELL TALENT AGENCY**
(AFTRA, SAG)
1700 Westlake Ave. N #600
Seattle, WA 98109
(206) 281-4646
Fax: (206) 281-5732

Contact: Lola Hallowell. The agency represents trained and experienced actors only, actively promoting them and encouraging them to do the same. Send picture and resume. No follow-up calls, please. If interested, the agency will call you for an audition.

■ **CAROL JAMES TALENT AGENCY** (AFTRA, SAG)
117 S Main St.
Seattle, WA 98104
(206) 447-9191
Fax: (206) 447-1501

Contact: Carol James. The Carol James Talent Agency has the highest percentage of SAG professionals of any agency in town (eighty percent of its 100 or so veteran actors), and is ranked as the toughest agency to break into in this market. Experienced adult performers only are invited to send photo/resume; no follow-up calls, please.

■ **ESI MODELS AND TALENT** (AFTRA, SAG)
600 Stewart St.
Seattle, WA 98101
(206) 448-2060
Fax: (206) 448-0536

Contact: Jerry & Eileen Seals. ESI is a progressive, selective agency representing some of Seattle's most exciting talent. Experienced Seattle professionals are invited to send photo/resume. No follow-up calls, please. The agent will respond if interested. (Formerly Eileen Seals.)

3.1 Talent Agents

■ **KID BIZ JTM** (AFTRA)
411 108th Ave. NE #2050
Bellevue, WA 98004
(206) 455-8800
Fax: (206) 646-9141

Contact: Jami Schwartz and Rod Stewart. Kid Biz has been representing kids and teens since 1988. New talent is accepted on an audition basis only; call for appointment and information, or send recent snapshot/resume.

■ **THE SEATTLE MODELS GUILD** (AFTRA, SAG)
1809 Seventh Ave. #303
Seattle, WA 98101
(206) 622-1406
Fax: (206) 622-8276

Contact: Kristy Meyers. Talent may send photo/resumes, but no follow-up calls, please. If interested, the agency will contact you. Also, open calls are held Mondays at 4 p.m.

■ **TEAM MODELS INTERNATIONAL** (AFTRA)
3431 - 96th Ave. NE
Bellevue, WA 98004
(206) 455-2969
Fax: (206) 455-2895

Contact: Leslie Birkland. Team Models represents talent ages 15 and older. The agency works in TV, film, commercial, print work and fashion shows. Send photos and resumes.

3.1 Talent Agents

■ **TOPO SWOPE TALENT AGENCY** (AFTRA)
1932 First Ave. #700
Seattle, WA 98101
(206) 443-2021
Fax: (206) 443-7648

Contact: Topo Swope. Topo Swope Talent is established as one of Seattle's leading agencies, providing clients with the Northwest's most exciting actors working in multimedia, interactive CD-Roms, commercials, film, TV, industrials, voice-overs, print and theater. Send photo/resume; follow-up calls are O.K.

Washington (Non-Union)

N.B. *The Actor's Handbook* does not recommend paying an agent for expensive photo packages. **For a list of recommended photographers and their going rates, please see 5.2 In a Supporting Role, Photographers** (prices range from $65 to $210).

■ **ABC KIDS AND TEENS**
10415 NE 37th Circle, Bldg.4
Kirkland, WA 98003
(206) 822-6339
Fax: (206) 822-5457

Contact: Debra Lukous. ABC Kids and Teens specializes in ages six months to 19 years. Please call for a new talent interview. All multicultural types are needed. No information was available as to whether ABC Kids and Teens recommends photo packages.

3.1 Talent Agents

■ COLLEEN BELL MODELING AND TALENT AGENCY
14205 SE 36ᵗʰ St. #100
Bellevue, WA 98006
(206) 649-1111
Fax: (206) 649-1113

Contact: Colleen Bell. A new agency, Colleen Bell represents children to young adults (ages 18 months to 24 years) for acting in film, commercials. television, video, industrials and voice-overs. The agency prefers that talent submit snapshots; it also has an open call once a month — please call for details. Photo packages are available from the agency for approximately $400, but it will accept previous pictures, if they are acceptable.

■ DREZDEN INTERNATIONAL MODELING AGENCY
N 3121 Division
Spokane, WA 99207
(509) 326-6800
Fax: (509) 327-0414

The Drezden International Modeling Agency represents clients doing runway work, print ads and television commercials. The agency offers photo packages to clients ranging from $350, paid to the agency.

■ EDGE MANAGEMENT
911 E Pike #210
Seattle, WA 98122
(206) 860-8874
Fax: (206) 860-8982

Contact: Michelle Marshall. This new full-service agency welcomes photos/resumes from all types; no follow up calls.

3.1 Talent Agents

■ **ENTCO INTERNATIONAL**
23607 Highway 99, #1D
Edmonds, WA 98026
(206) 670-0888
Fax: (206) 670-0777

Entco is a full-service agency representing older children and adults for TV, film commercials, industrials, voice-overs, print and stand-up. It accepts photos/ resumes from all types. Please, no drop-ins or follow-up calls. The agency does not offer photo packages; clients choose their own photographers.

■ **EMERALD CITY MODEL & TALENT**
1980 Harvard Ave. E
Seattle, WA 98102
(206) 742-7340; (206) 329-7768

Contact: John Harb. Emerald City Model & Talent offers clients photo packages, paid to the agency. Information regarding price was unavailable at the time of publication.

■ **THE KIM BROOKE GROUP MODEL & TALENT MANAGEMENT**
2044 Eastlake Ave. E
Seattle, WA 98102
(206) 329-1111
Fax: (206) 328-5177

Contact: Kimberly Brooke. In business for 15 years, the Kim Brooke agency either recommends photographers or offers modest photo packages for clients averaging about $125 for a basic headshot photo shoot. Clients are encouraged to find their own photographer; purchasing a photo package through the agency is not required for representation. Kim Brooke welcomes clients of all ages; send a photo/resume. Follow-up calls are acceptable.

3.1 Talent Agents

■ MDF AGENCY
13606 NE 20th # 303
Bellevue, WA 98005
(206) 562-9893
Fax: (206) 643-3260

Contact: Michael Fields. MDF is a new agency for commercials, voice-over work and extra work. Call to set up an appointment. They prefer that you do not send a photo-resume; the agency has its own photographer. Headshots are not required, but there is a one-time $30 fee.

■ MATURE TALENT ENTERPRISES
620 Fifth Ave. W #109
Seattle, WA 98119
Tel & Fax: (206) 283-3367

Contact: Mozelle Sims. This is the Northwest's only talent agency devoted exclusively to supplying mature (age 45 +) talent for film, TV corporate video, commercials and voice-overs. The agency does not offer photo packages per se, but there is a charge for copying headshots, as well as a $260 portfolio fee paid to the agency.

■ NFI TALENT/NORTHWEST KIDS
19009 - 33rd Ave. W #100
Lynnwood, WA 98036
(206) 775-8385
Fax: (206) 771-1114

Contact: Alayna Sheron. NFI Talent specializes in film extra casting, commercials and voice-overs. Qualified talent of all ages should send photos/resumes. Please, no follow-up calls. No photo packages are offered by the agency; talents picks their own photographers.

■ PASCUCCI NW MODELS
625 Commerce St. #130
Tacoma, WA 98402
(206) 572-0994

Contact: Christina Pascucci. Pascucci is actively seeking talent between the ages of two and 65 for work in commercials, film theatre and video. Multicultural talent is welcome. Since Ms. Pascucci "does not take kickbacks from photographers," photo packages are not offered, although referrals are made. (Average cost is $50.)

■ TERRY TERRY TALENT MANAGEMENT
P.O. Box 77310
Seattle, WA 98177
(206) 546-4376
Fax: (206) 546-4957

Established in the Northwest for 11 years, Terry Terry represents both non-union and union actors for commercial, industrial, television and feature film work. Send photo/resume. No information was available concerning photo packages.

■ TERRY TERRY WEST
820 Pacific # 201
Bremerton, WA 98337
(360) 373-5283
Fax: (360) 415-9052

Terry Terry Talent Management-West represents talent for film, commercial, corporate, industrial, interactive media, TV and print. Call or write. Terry Terry requested that we did "not publish anything about their photo packages."

3.1 Talent Agents

■ THOMPSON MEDIA TALENT
11522 - 24th Ave. NE
Seattle, WA 98125
(206) 363-5555
Fax: (206)363-0594

Contact: Scott Thompson. In business for nearly 40 years, Thompson Media Talent represents a diverse selection of quality actors for film, television, voice-over, industrial, CD-Rom, interactive and some print work. Actors are encouraged to send photos/resumes; follow-up calls are welcomed. They have a list of photographers that they can refer clients to, but they do not offer any sort of photo package.

■ THE WARD AGENCY
17506-69th Place West
Edmonds, WA 98026
(206) 787-1982
Fax: (206) 787-5818

Contact: Helene Ward represents new and experienced talent for TV, film, commercials, corporate video, print, CD-Rom and voice-overs. Send photos/resumes. Absolutely no photo packages; the agency strongly urges new talent to shop around.

■ YOUNG PERFORMER MANAGEMENT
124 N 103rd St.
Seattle, WA 98133
(206) 989-9080
Fax: (206) 789-2370

Contact: Donnajeane Goheen. A small, select agency, Young Performer Management represents ethnically diverse children ages three to 17 for commercials and film work. Currently, Young Performers is especially looking for boys age 4 to 8. Send photos/resumes with covering letter. Periodic open calls are held. No photo packages are offered.

3.1 Talent Agents

<u>Oregon (Union Franchised)</u>

■ **ACTORS ONLY** (AFTRA)
3430 SE Belmont St. #204
Portland, OR 97214
(503) 233-5073
Fax: (503) 223-6865

    Contact: Monica Rodriguez. Actors only, a small, full-service agency specializing in "personal attention to top professionals," books film, television, industrials, multimedia, live performances and trade shows. Send photos/resumes; follow-up calls are O.K.

■ **CUSICK'S AGENCY** (AFTRA)
1009 NW Hoyt #100
Portland, OR 97209
(503) 274-8555
Fax: (503) 274-4615

    Contact: Chris Cusick. An AFTRA signatory since 1988, Cusick's is a leading agency for voice-over, film and television. Send photo/resume. Follow-up calls are O.K.

■ **ERHART TALENT** (AFTRA)
037 SW Hamilton
Portland, OR 97201
(503) 243-6362
Fax: (503) 243-1460

    Contact: Lo Erhart or Lynn Sagen. Erhart Talent is an actor's agency representing actors and voices for film, commercial, industrial and interactive media. Send photo/resume;no calls, please. (Formerly Wilson.)

3.1 Talent Agents

■ **RYAN ARTISTS INC.** (AFTRA)
239 NW 13th Ave. #215
Portland, OR 97209
(503) 274-1005
Fax: (503) 274-0907

Contact: Stacey Spencer. Ryan Artists is a full-service agency representing actors and models in films, television, commercials, multimedia and industrials. Send photo/ resume.

Oregon (Non-Union)

■ **ABC KIDS AND TEENS TALENT MANAGEMENT**
3829 NE Tillamook
Portland, OR 97212
(503) 249-2945
Fax: (503) 249-7429

Contact: Carol Lukens. ABC represents infants to age 21 breaking into TV, film and print. ABC provides photo packages for between $125 and $445. Call for new talent interviews.

■ **PRO TALENT INC.**
921 SW Morrison, #301
Portland, OR 97205
(503) 228-9317
Fax: (503) 228-5649

Contact: Tanya Leedy, Film Division. Pro talent is looking for actors for industrials, commercials, film, television, interactive media and print. Send photos/ resume, or call. No photo packages are offered by Pro Talent, who characterize themselves as "personable, aggressive, innovative and ethical."

3.1 Talent Agents

■ TALENT MANAGEMENT ASSOCIATES
1574 Coburg Rd #143
Eugene, OR 97401
(541) 345-1525
Fax: (541) 687-9790

Contact: Gloria Clow. TMA represents actors for film, television, commercials, industrials and voice-overs, and radio. Please send photos/resumes and demo tapes for consideration.

Multicultural Agents

■ DIAMOND KIDS
4126 - 46th Ave. S
Seattle, WA 98118
(206) 723-7704
Fax: (206) 725-6223

Contact: Michelle Williams. In business for two years, Diamonds Kids represents primarily, but not exclusively, ethnic children. Send photo/resume; follow-up calls are O.K. Photo packages are not offered.

CASTING DIRECTORS

Washington

■ **A & M CASTING ASSOCIATES**
10415 NE 37th Circle
Kirkland, WA 98033
(206) 822-6339
Fax: (206) 822-5457

(See A & M Casting Associates under Casting Directors, Oregon.)

■ **COMPLETE CASTING BY STEPHEN SALAMUNOVICH**
2019 Third Ave. #205
Seattle, WA 98121
(206) 441-5058

This full-service casting company welcomes photos and resumes; mail submission only, please. No drop-ins. Auditions are conducted by appointment. General interviews are conducted as the schedule allows.

■ **CASTING BY WALKER & COMPANY**
603 Stewart St.
Seattle, WA 98101
(206) 622-9646
Fax: (206) 448-4449

Contact: Heidi Lee Walker. This is a full-service casting agency. Send photo/resume before calling for an interview appointment.

3.2   Casting Directors

■ CASTING REAL PEOPLE
234 - 12th Ave. E
Seattle, WA 98102
(206) 322-5855
Fax: (206) 328-7002

Contact: Kerry Loewen. A full-service agency, Casting Real People is looking for absolutely all types. Send photo/resume as well as video audition tape.

■ CHERYL HONEY CASTING SERVICES
21902 Second Ave. W
Bothell, WA 98021
(206) 487-4009
Fax: (206) 455-4821

Cheryl specializes in casting real people and in talent-scouting. No follow-up calls, please.

■ KALLES-LEVINE PRODUCTIONS
506 Second Ave. #1525
Smith Tower
Seattle, WA 98104
(206) 447-9318

Contact: Patti Kalles or Laurie Levine. A full-service casting agency, Kalles-Levine welcomes photos/resumes. Interviews are available to talent with previous stage and/or commercial experience. Follow-up calls are O.K.

■ PRODUCCIONES PINO
2609 198th Place SW
Lynnwood, WA 98036
(206) 774-7772
Fax: (206) 775-1980

A specialized casting agency that casts all multiethnic actors and those with foreign language skills. The agency accepts photo/resumes and follow-up calls.

3.2 Casting Directors

■ JODI ROTHFIELD CASTING ASSOCIATES, CSA
2033 Sixth Ave. #306
Seattle, WA 98121
(206) 448-0927
Fax: (206) 448-1016

Contact: Jodi Rothfield and Cate Macapia. This full-service casting agency welcomes photos/resumes by mail. Actors are invited to send comp tickets for current stage productions. Call for information on general auditions and classes. "Actors are always welcome!"

Oregon

■ A & M CASTING ASSOCIATES
3829 NE Tillamook
Portland, OR 97212
Tel & Fax: (503) 255-3785
(503) 249-2949 (message center)

Contact: Carol Lukiens. A & M handles film and commercial work, and welcomes photos/resumes from experienced stage and commercial talent. No follow-up calls; postcards are O.K.

■ BARBARA BALSZ CASTING
4710 SW 47th Ave.
Portland, OR 97221
Tel & Fax: (503) 245-6343

Contact: Barbara Balsz. Complete casting services for film, TV, commercials and industrials.

3.2   Casting Directors

■ **MEGANN RATZOW CASTING**
P.O. Box 15056
Portland, OR 97293
(503) 251-9050

Contact: Megann Ratzow. The agency casts principals for movies, commercials and industrial films. It welcomes photos/resumes; no follow-up calls, please.

■ **NANETTE TROUTMAN CASTING, CSA**
1110 SW Salmon
Portland, OR 97205
(503) 241-4233
Fax: (503) 241-4230

Contact: Nanette Troutman. Feature films, TV series and movies of the week are Troutman's forte. Although Troutman works primarily through agents, she welcomes photos/resumes from actors without representation. No follow-up calls, please.

■ **PAM GILLES CASTING**
815 NW 13th #C
Portland, OR 97209
(503) 227-2656
Fax: (503) 233-7285

Contact: Pam Gilles. This is a full-service casting agency. Send photos/resumes, voice-over and audition tapes. Follow-up calls are O.K., but Gilles prefers drop-ins.

CORPORATE VIDEO

Washington

■ **ARCHDIOCESE OF SEATTLE**
910 Marion St.
Seattle, WA 98104
(206) 382-4826

Educational and commercial TV programming. Uses mostly non-union voice and on-camera talent. Send photo/resume/tapes to the video communications manager.

■ **BOEING VIDEO SERVICES**
P.O. Box 3707/MS 6Y-66
Seattle, WA 98124-2207
(206) 393-7702

Contact: Doug Dawson. The Northwest's busiest corporate video department produces some 700 video and film projects a year (for training, marketing, sales, etc.). Many are voice-over projects. Boeing producers depend mostly on agency talent, but frequently call upon the company's own talent bank. Working professionals are invited to send a photo/resume and tape (including non-broadcast samples).

N.B. The in-house producers described in this section include only those that have expressed an interest in hearing directly from the acting community. Those not listed deal directly with agents or casting directors.

3.3 Corporate Video

■ **BON MARCHE**
3rd Ave. and Pine St.
Seattle, WA 98181
(206) 506-7578

Contact: Broadcast Production Manager, Bill Blanchard, for radio and television commercials; uses both union and non-union talent. Send photos/resume and video/audio tapes for industrial videos. Contact: Mary Jean Stephens for Special Events (singers, comedians, child entertainers, etc.).

■ **FARMERS NEW WORLD LIFE**
3003 77th Ave. SE
Mercer Island, WA 98040
(206) 232-8400

Contact: Kevin Allar. Training videos and product introductions; works with non-union voice-over and on-camera talent. Accepts photo/resumes, voice and video reels. No phone calls, please.

■ **LTC, INC.**
2 Union Sq., 22nd Floor
601 Union St.
Seattle, WA 98101-2363
(206) 223-0938

Contact: Nancy Griffith. Corporate video production for GE Capitol Assurance, including training films, some commercials, informational videos, video magazines, etc. Send photo/resumes, voice and videotapes. No phone calls, please.

■ **PUGET POWER**
P.O. Box 97034
Bellevue, WA 98009-9734
(206) 454-6363

Contact: Chris Nardine. Produces videos for training, marketing and shareholder purposes. Uses on-

3.3 Corporate Video

camera and voice talent, sometimes union. Keeps active talent file; welcomes photo/resumes and tapes. Has paid AFTRA scale.

■ **SEATTLE CITY LIGHT**
1015 Third Ave. #809
Seattle, WA 98104
(206) 684-3008

Contact: Sharon Bennett. Produces training and recruiting videos. Accepts photo/resumes and tapes. Send to the attention of the video coordinator.

■ **UNIVERSITY OF WASHINGTON**
Box 353090 Video Production/Dept. UW TV
Seattle, WA 98195
(206) 543-3800

Contact: Jim Lorang or Chris Latham. This department handles all of the video production services for the University. They produce documentaries, dramas, work related to academic subject matter, reportage of research work, etc. The scope of their work is broad, ranging from a drama about AIDS prevention to the PSAs which run during half-time at football and basketball games. Send photo/resume. No phone calls, please.

■ **US WEST COMMUNICATIONS**
Creative Services Dept.
1600 Bell Plaza #2703
Seattle, WA 98191
(206) 345-8928

Contact: Jay Watland. Training and marketing videos; generally works through agencies, but not exclusively. Accepts photo/resumes, voice tapes and non-broadcast video samples.

3.3 Corporate Video

■ **WASHINGTON NATURAL GAS**
815 Mercer St.
Seattle, WA 98109
(206) 224-2286

Contact: Chris Nardine. Produces videos for training, marketing, educational and shareholder purposes. Uses on-camera and voice talent. Keeps active talent file; welcomes photo/resumes and tapes. Has paid AFTRA scale.

Oregon

■ **FREIGHTLINER CORPORATION**
4747 N Channel Ave.
Portland, OR 97217
(503) 735-8000

Contact: Don Stait. Marketing, training and customer videos for truck manufacturer. Works with Portland and Seattle talent, pays AFTRA scale and maintains an active bank of photos and tapes. Follow-up calls O.K.

■ **NORTHWEST NATURAL GAS**
220 NW Second Ave.
Portland, OR 97209
(503) 226-4211 ext. 3505

Contact: Jacque Wehrle. Marketing and training videos; most projects are voice-overs. Send tapes to the PR Department; photos and resumes to the Advertising Department, which handles TV spots and PSAs.

■ **NORTH WILLIAMETTE TELECOM**
P.O. Box 850
Canby, OR 97013
(503) 263-8080

Contact: Kathy Weddle. Primarily work on television commercials; most projects are voice-overs. Send photos/resume, tapes. Follow-up calls okay.

3.3 Corporate Video

■ **OREGON CUTTING SYSTEMS**
4909 SE International Way
Portland, OR 97222-4679
(503) 653-4511

Contact: Rick Morehouse. Training, safety and
marketing videos for manufacturing products; maintains
talent bank of photos and tapes. Send to the advertising
manager.

■ **D.O.T. PHOTO & VIDEO SERVICES**
355 Capital St. NE
Salem, OR 97310-1354
(503) 986-3702

Contact: Ted Burney. They are a corporate/
industrial production house specializing in work for
government agencies. Oregon D.O.T. is their largest client,
although they do work for other government agencies
upon request. They are looking primarily for industrial
standups. This work is sometimes of a detailed technical
nature; mainly location shoots. Quarterly projects are
possible. D.O.T. maintains an active talent file and refers
talent to other government agencies. Send name, phone
number and availability. Follow-up calls okay.

■ **PACIFICORP ELECTRIC SYSTEMS**
Attn.: Video Production
920 SW Sixth Ave. (650-PFFC)
Portland, OR 97204
(503) 464-6280

Contact: Rodger Shervey. Training, safety, and
marketing videos; usually draws on agency voice and
camera talent, but does maintain an active talent bank.

3.3 Corporate Video

■ **PORTLAND FIRE BUREAU**
Television Services
2915 SE 13th Pl.
Portland, OR 97202
(503) 823-3911

Contact: Kent Powloski. Live and taped programming for Portland-area firefighters; includes safety and training videos, documentaries, PSAs and an in-house video magazine. Limited use of professional talent, but photos and tapes accepted.

■ **PORTLAND PUBLIC SCHOOLS**
5210 N Kirby
Portland, OR 97217
(503) 916-5838

Contact: Joanne Hatch. Instructional video for the Portland Public School District. Send photos/resumes. No phone calls, please.

■ **TEKTRONIX**
TV/Media Services
P.O. Box 500/MS 74115
Beaverton, OR 97077-0001
(503) 627-2368

Contact: Tom Dietz. Manufactures electronic measurement devices; annually produces 90 to 100 marketing, training, new product and in-house communication videos. Works with Portland and Seattle talent, and maintains an active bank of photos and tapes.

PRODUCTION COMPANIES

Washington

■ **AUDISEE**
1011 Western Ave. #506
Seattle, WA 98104
(206) 382-1901
Fax: (206) 382-1931

■ **GREAT NORTHERN MEDIA GROUP, INC.**
300 Fairview Ave. N
Seattle, WA 98101
(206) 625-1000
Fax: (206) 382-9200

Film and video production, both corporate and commercial work. Maintains active talent file.

■ **HOT SHOT PRODUCTIONS**
2223 Second Ave.
Seattle, WA 98121
(206) 682-6300
Fax: (206) 441-0743

■ **LON GIBBY PRODUCTIONS**
E 113 Magnesium Rd. #B
Spokane, WA 99208
(509) 467-1113
(206) 624-4268 (Seattle)

Corporate videos 70%, commercials 30%; works with Seattle and Portland talent, and maintains active files. Calls OK.

N.B. The production companies described in this section include only those that have expressed a desire to hear directly from the acting community. Those not listed deal directly with agents and casting directors.

3.4 Production

■ **MARDIG & COMPANY**
3817 - 29th W
Seattle, WA 98199
(206) 283-4252

    Commercials 70%, corporate videos 30%; maintains an active talent file.

■ **MERWIN PRODUCTIONS**
419 Occidental Ave. S #208
Seattle, WA 98104
(206) 621-7552

    Mostly corporate videos; maintains an active talent bank of photos, resumes and tapes.

■ **NORTH BY NORTHWEST PRODUCTIONS**
903 W Broadway
Spokane, WA 99201
(509) 324-2949

■ **RXL PULITZER**
East 4022 Broadway
Spokane, WA 99202
(509) 536-7919

    Video production and telecommunications; maintains an active talent file.

■ **PRODUCCIONES PINO**
2609 - 198th Place SW
Lynnwood, WA 98036-6986
(206) 774-7772

    Producciones Pino does a variety of production work, including foreign language material.

3.4 Production

■ **PURE AUDIO**
2908 First Ave.
Seattle, WA 98121
(206) 728-6300
Fax: (206)728-1433

■ **SCHORR COMMUNICATION, INC.**
1109 First Ave. #400
Seattle, WA 98101
(206) 233-0135
Fax: (206) 233-0236

■ **VIDEOCAST MEDIA PRODUCTIONS**
Box 639
Freeland, WA 98249
(206) 454-0902

Oregon

■ **BLASHFIELD & ASSOCIATES**
1801 NW Upshur #210
Portland, OR 97219
(503) 228-0570
Fax: (503) 228-2322

■ **CREATIVE MEDIA DEVELOPMENT**
1732 NW Quimby
Portland, OR 97209
(503) 223-6794
Fax: (503) 223-2430

■ **EMA VIDEO PRODUCTIONS** (AFTRA)
1306 NW Hoyt #101
Portland, OR 97209
(503) 241-8663
Fax: (503) 224-6967

■ **ODYSSEY PRODUCTIONS INC.**
2800 NW Thurman St.
Portland, OR 97210
(503) 223-3480
Fax: (503) 223-3493

■ **DAVID POULSHOCK PRODUCTIONS INC.**
1231 NW Hoyt St. #305
Portland, OR 97209
(503) 228-7576
Fax: (503) 228-7775

■ **WESTCOM CREATIVE GROUP**
2295 Coburg Rd. #105
Eugene, OR 97401
(541) 484-4314

■ **WILL VINTON STUDIOS**
1400 NW 22nd Ave.
Portland, OR 97210
(503) 225-1130
Fax: (503) 226-3746

Uses mostly voice talent, but invites photos and resumes for frequent special projects.

ADVERTISING AGENCIES

Washington

■ **AUGUSTAVO BURRUS**
601 Aurora Ave. N #207
Seattle, WA 98109
(206) 281-3550

■ **BALLARD BRATSBURG** (AFTRA)
506 Second Ave. W
Seattle, WA 98119
(206) 284-8800

■ **BREMS EASTMAN**
3131 Elliot Ave. #280
Seattle, WA 98121
(206) 284-9400

■ **CF2GS**
1008 Western Ave. #201
Seattle, WA 98104
(206) 223-6464

■ **THE COMMUNICATIONS GROUP** (AFTRA)
40 Lake Bellevue #100
Bellevue, WA 98005
(206) 453-5252

N.B. While this roster is by no means a complete list of
Washington agencies, the ones included here were chosen not
only for their size but because TV and radio commercials
represented at least 30% of their business. Address photos,
pictures and voice tapes to the agency's "broadcast coordinator."

■ **ELGIN SYFERD/DDB NEEDHAM** (AFTRA)
1008 Western Ave. #601
Seattle, WA 98104-1032
(206) 442-9900

■ **EVANS GROUP** (AFTRA)
190 Queen Anne Ave. N
Seattle, WA 98109
(206) 285-2222

■ **EVERGREEN MEDIA INC.**
21010 - 76th Ave. W
Edmonds, WA 98026
(206) 771-0988

■ **HINTON & STEEL, INC.** (AFTRA)
87 Wall St.
Seattle, WA 98121
(206) 441-3455

■ **JAY RAY ADS & PR**
736 Broadway
Tacoma, WA 98402
(206) 627-9128

■ **ROBIDEAUX, & ASSOCIATES**
W 926 Sprague Ave. #582
Spokane, WA 99204
(509) 838-1036

■ **SMITH, PHILLIPS, & DiPIETRO**
1440 N 16th Ave. #1
Yakima, WA 98902
(509) 248-1760

■ **STAUNTON AND EVERYBODY**
1809 Seventh Ave. #1600
Seattle, WA 98101
(206) 224-4242

3.5 Ad Agencies

■ **WHITERUNKLE ASSOCIATES**
505 W Riverside #300
Spokane, WA 99201
(509) 747-6767

Oregon

■ **BOAZ GROUP**
2207 NE Broadway
Portland, OR 97232
(503) 287-1383

■ **BORDERS PERRIN & NORRANDER** (AFTRA)
222 SW Yamhill St.
Portland, OR 97204
(503) 227-2506

■ **CAPELLI MILES WILTZ KELLY**
101 SW Main St. #1905
Portland, OR 97204
(503) 241-1515
or
199 E Fifth Ave. #25
Eugene, OR 97401
(503) 484-1515

■ **THE COATES AGENCY, INC.**
320 SW Oak #300
Portland, OR 97204
(503) 241-1124

■ **DAVIS, BALL & COLOMBATTO**
101 SW Main St. #300
Portland, OR 97204
(503) 241-7781

3.5 Ad Agencies

■ **DEWITZ DEWITZ ROUZEE**
516 SE Morrison #300
Portland, OR 97214
(503) 238-0611

■ **GARD STRANG, EDWARDS & ALDRIDGE**
1200 NW Front #220
Portland, OR 97209
(503) 226-2721

■ **GERBER ADVERTISING**
209 SW Oak St.
Portland, OR 97204
(503) 221-0100

■ **GILCHRIST & ASSOCIATES**
319 SW Washington, Mezz. Level
Portland, OR 97204
(503) 243-1030

■ **GLOBAL EVENTS GROUP**
P.O. Box 3024
Portland, OR 97208
(503) 232-3000

■ **THE HALLOCK AGENCY INC.**
2445 NW Irving St.
Portland, OR 97210
(503) 224-1711

■ **HARRIS, MASSEY, HERINCKX**
2020 SW Fourth Ave. #900
Portland, OR 97201
(503) 295-1922

■ **INS ADVERTISING**
811 NW 19th
Portland, OR 97209
(503) 221-5000

3.5 Ad Agencies

■ **JOHNSON SHEEN**
215 NW Park Ave.
Portland, WA 97209
(503) 222-4117

■ **KNOLL & COMPANY**
110 SW Yamhill #300
Portland, OR 97204
(503) 226-2867

■ **LIVENGOOD & COMPANY**
806 SW Broadway #800
Portland, OR 97205
(503) 225-0437

■ **THE MANDALA AGENCY**
709 NW Wall St.
Bend, OR 97701
(541) 389-6344

■ **PARMA ADVERTISING**
13700 NW Science Park Dr.
Portland, OR 97229
(503) 644-2666

■ **ROBLEY MARKETING**
700 SW Taylor #400
Portland, OR 97205
(503) 279-4000

■ **RYAN HUTCHINS ARTHUR SOUTHWICK**
4386 SW Macadam Ave. #301
Portland, OR 97201
(503) 227-5547

■ **SULLIVAN PATTISON CLEVENGER**
219 SW Stark #200
Portland, OR 97204
(503) 226-4553

■ **PRIDEAUX SWEARINGEN**
2311 NW Irving St.
Portland, OR 97210
(503) 228-1151

■ **MARY R. TAHAN ADVERTISING**
1020 SW Taylor St. #360
Portland, OR 97205
(503) 227-6700

■ **THOMPSON & HUFFSCHMIDT**
208 SW First #240
Portland, OR 97204
(503) 224-5384

■ **TURTLEDOVE CLEMENS INC.**
735 E First Ave.
Portland, OR 97204
(503) 226-3581

■ **WIEDEN & KENNEDY INC.**
320 SW Washington St.
Portland, OR 97204
(503) 228-4381

VOICE/CAMERA OPPORTUNITIES

Seattle

■ **GLOBE RADIO REPERTORY COMPANY**
(AFTRA)
5220 University Ave. NE
Seattle, WA 98105
(206) 682-6882

For more than 10 years, Globe has remained committed to producing national radio drama, usually only one show per year, depending on funding. Globe prefers talent with previous mic experience. They pay AFTRA scale for both rehearsals and performance. Check the Equity Hotline for audition information.

■ **JACK STRAW PRODUCTIONS** (AFTRA)
4261 Roosevelt Way NE
Seattle, WA 98105
(206) 634-0919
Fax:(206) 634-0925

Contact: Joan Rabinowitz. Jack Straw produces radio dramas using area talent on a project-by-project basis, sometimes paid. Watch the newspaper callboards for auditions.

■ **WASHINGTON TALKING BOOK AND BRAILLE LIBRARY**
821 Lenora
Seattle, WA 98121-2783
v/TDD (206) 464-6930
Fax: 464-0247

This state-supported library supplies live and pre-recorded radio programming and mailed book tapes to listeners throughout Washington State. Volunteers are needed year-round to tape fiction and nonfiction reading matter, and to provide news and entertainment programming for its closed-circuit FM radio outlet. If interested, ask for Volunteer Services.

Public Access Television

■ **SUMMIT CABLEVISION**
4316 S 104th Pl.
Seattle, WA 98178
(206) 865-0052

Contact: Jerry Fernandez. South Seattle cable TV operator; it provides "citizen producers" with 3/4" and video training, studio facilities and access to the Public Access Channel. Workshops, instruction and editing equipment are all free for public access use.

■ **TCI, INC.**   **TCI, ROOSEVELT**
1125 N 98th St.   8914 Roosevelt Way NE
Seattle, WA 98103   Seattle, WA 98115
(206) 522-6672   (206) 527-5323
Fax: (206) 528-8049   Fax: (206)523-5910

Contact: Ken Harris. Seattle's major cable TV franchise; it provides "citizen producers" with an opportunity to work with the variety of facilities found in a mid-sized commercial station. Training is available in video production and in equipment use (½" cameras, editing)at two locations. All productions are aired on the Public Access channel. Call about TCI's orientation meeting. Only the N 98th Street location has a studio available; the Roosevelt location only provides equipment for remote or location shots. Contact John, Patty or Ray for the Roosevelt office.

VOICE-OVER PRODUCTION

Seattle, Portland

■ **ADS RECORDING**
215 SW Hooker St.
Portland, OR 97201
(503) 223-9941
Fax: (503) 223-6073

Contact: Ryan Wiley. Audio production; primarily radio commercials. Send tapes; no follow-up calls, please.

■ **AUDISEE**
1011 Western Ave. #506
Seattle, WA 98104
(206) 382-1901
Fax: (206) 382-1931

Contact: Susan McArthur. Audio production; Audisee works in radio, TV and non-broadcast markets. Maintains an active bank of voice tapes, and distributes a company reel.

■ **AVCON MEDIA SOLUTIONS** (AFTRA)
121 Stewart St. # 205
Seattle, WA 98101
(206) 441-7556
Fax: (206) 728-4054

Multi-image productions. Produces video/slide shows for corporate clients. Prefers voice talent with non-broadcast experience. Send tapes and resume.

3.7 Voice-Over

■ **BAD ANIMALS/SEATTLE** (AFTRA)
2212 Fourth Ave.
Seattle, WA 98121
(206) 443-1500
Fax: (206) 441-2910

Contact: Kris Dangla. Seattle's ranking commercial recording studio; distributes a current Seattle voice reel, and welcomes tapes from experienced talent. Send cassettes. (Formerly Steve Lawson Productions.)

■ **CLATTER & DIN INC.**
1505 Western Ave. #600
Seattle, WA 98101
(206) 464-0520
Fax: (206) 464-0702

Contact: Lisa Myron. Audio production in radio, TV and non-broadcast markets. Maintains active bank of voice tapes. Send tapes & resumes.

■ **DIGITAL ONE/PACE VIDEO CENTER**
2020 SW Fourth, 7th Floor
Portland, OR 97201
(503) 226-7223
Fax: (503) 224-7413

Contact: Michael Carter. Post-production studio; provides narration for a wide variety of commercial and non-broadcast videos. Portland and Seattle voice talent are encouraged to send tapes/resumes to the audio department.

3.7 Voice-Over

■ **EARFORCE, INC.**
315 Terry Ave. N
Seattle, WA 98109
(206) 467-4844
Fax: (206) 467-0886

Contact: Brook Watkins. Earforce produces TV and radio commercials, and maintains an active bank of voice tapes. Send resumes and tapes, but no follow-up calls, please.

■ **THE GLENN SOUND CO, INC**
228 Dexter Ave. N
Seattle, WA 98109
(206) 583-8112
Fax: (206) 483-0930

Contact: Glenn Lorbiecki. Produces radio & TV commercials, sound design for film, multimedia for corporations, etc. Maintains an active voice-tape bank. Send tapes and resumes, but no follow-up calls, please.

■ **HEADBONE INTERACTIVE**
1520 Bellevue Ave.
Seattle, WA 98122
(206) 323-0073

Headbone Interactive produces children's interactive software. Although they do use agents, they are interested in maintaining a talent file.

■ **HOYT'S GREATER RADIO COMMUNITY**
11414 Eighth Ave. NW
Seattle, WA 98177
(206) 298-4945
Fax: (206) 363-4973

Greater Radio writes and produces radio commercials; an award-winning creative radio company that uses union and non-union voice talent, and works on accounts in the Northwest and across the nation.

■ **IRONWOOD STUDIOS**
601 NW 80th St.
Seattle, WA 98117
(206) 789-7569
Fax: (206)784-2880

Contact: Paul Scoles. Maintains an active talent bank;
welcomes resumes and cassettes. About 40% of its output
is radio/TV and non-broadcast voice tracks. Send tapes
and resumes.

■ **STEVE LAWSON PRODUCTIONS** (AFTRA)

(See Bad Animals/Seattle above.)

■ **LEW'S RECORDING PLACE** (AFTRA)
1219 Westlake Ave. N #115
Seattle, WA 98109
(206) 285-7550

Contact: Stephen Jones. Works in film, radio, TV and
non-broadcast market. Also produces corporate voice
cassettes. Welcomes resumes and cassettes. No follow-
up calls, please.

■ **MACDONALD RECORDING COMPANY**
(AFTRA)

(See Pure Audio Recording below.)

■ **PURE AUDIO RECORDING** (AFTRA)
2908 First Ave.
Seattle, WA 98121
(206) 728-6300
Fax: (206) 728-1433

Contact: Paul Goldberg.   A leading Seattle
commercial studio; produces radio/TV spots and a wide
variety of non-broadcast projects. Interested in hearing
from experienced voice talent. (Formerly MacDonald
Recording Company.)

3.7 Voice-Over

■ **REX RECORDING & VIDEO POST** (AFTRA)
1931 SE Morrison
Portland, OR 97214
(503) 238-4525
Fax: (503) 236-8347

Contact: Greg Branson. Major commercial production studio; maintains an active bank of commercial and non-broadcast voice tapes.

■ **SCREAM MUSIC**
422 SW 13th Ave.
Portland, OR 97205
(503) 221-5737
Fax: (503) 221-2036

Contact: Minervini. Commercial music production; maintains an active talent bank for commercial and slide-show projects. Interested in hearing both commercial and non-broadcast voice samples.

■ **STUDIO 5**
13400 Northup Way #2
Bellevue, WA 98005
(206) 643-1755
Fax: (206) 641-2522

Contact: Becky McPeters. Audio for video; demo tapes; radio commercials. Send tapes/resumes; no follow-up calls, please.

MEDIA ORGANIZATIONS

Regional

■ **AFTRA/SEATTLE**
601 Valley St. #100
Seattle, WA 98109
(206) 282-2506

Seattle's branch of the American Federation of
Television and Radio Artists is ranked, in terms of size, as
one of the top ten in the country. Due to a sharp influx of
TV/film projects, Seattle is also one of the country's busiest
commercial acting centers. Local AFTRA membership
fluctuates between 1,000 and 1,100 (about 85% of whom
are free-lance). As of November 1, 1996, the AFTRA office
will have a SAG representative.

The Local has also implemented a "conservatory"
program, offering free professional workshops such as
"Meet the Casting Director" to its members.

■ **AFTRA/PORTLAND**
516 SE Morrison #M3
Portland, OR 97214
(503) 238-6914

A small, but increasingly busy regional market,
AFTRA/Portland has over 400 members, two-thirds of
whom are free-lancers. There are four major AFTRA talent
agencies and many signatory companies. Although the
growth taking place in the late 1980's has slowed down,
the Portland market has been holding its own through
these difficult times. SAG will have a representative in
the Portland AFTRA office as of November 1, 1996.

3.8 Media

■ **NORTHWEST FILM CENTER**
1219 SW Park Ave.
Portland, OR 97205
(503) 221-1156

Sponsors of the Northwest Film and Video Festival, the Portland International Film Festival and an ongoing program of film screenings, this is also about the only non-university setting in the Northwest in which to study film-making (as well as video). A full schedule of classes is available, including: 16mm production and editing, video production and editing, animation and writing.

■ **911 MEDIA ARTS CENTER**
117 Yale Ave. N
Seattle, WA 98109
(206) 682-6552
Fax: (206) 682-7422

911 Media Arts Center encourages and supports independent media artists from the Seattle area and worldwide, and has made a concerted effort in recent months toward involvement with the Seattle theatre community. The center offers workshops in the use of video and film equipment, grant writing and performance art to members (and non-members, at slightly higher prices).

■ **SCREEN ACTORS GUILD (SAG)**

(See AFTRA, this section.)

■ **WASHINGTON STATE FILM AND VIDEO OFFICE**
2001 6th Ave. #2600
Seattle, WA 98121
(206) 464-7148

Contact: Kristina Ericson, Cathy Sander or Suzy Kellett. The Washington State Film and Video Office, a division of the Department of Trade and Economic

3.8 Media

Development, works to promote Washington state as a desirable location for out-of-state film production. The office acts as a liaison between production companies and local governmental and private agencies, and can help with getting the proper permits. In addition, they keep photo files of cities, towns, historic sites and general geography, and will gladly answer any questions about film production in the state of Washington. Recently, a jobline has been added for talent and extras which also includes Cautions and Guidelines, letting actors know their rights (see 1.1 Calendar). The jobline number is (206) 464-6074.

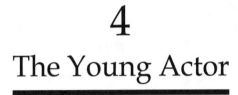

4
The Young Actor

ACTING COACHES/STAGE

Seattle

■ **CONNIE SPONHEIM BAUER** **(360) 568-2318**

Audition and performance skills coach for Grades 3-12; also conducts in-service drama workshops for teachers. Bauer is a working Seattle actor with a master's degree in acting/directing, and has teaching credentials for elementary and secondary grades. Snohomish.

■ **LANI BROCKMAN** **(206) 827-3123**

Lani Brockman is the director of Studio East, and trained in NY at Circle In The Square Theatre. She is a general coach as well as an audition coach, with lots of material for teens. 285-2589 or 654-0111.

■ **VICKY CARVER** **(206) 632-0201**
(Equity, SAG, AFTRA)

Audition coach for middle and high school drama students; currently teaches English and Drama at Seattle's Nathan Hale HS. Carver is a Juilliard-trained stage performer.

■ **CATE KOLER** **(206) 935-9782**

Koler coaches students in audition techniques and basic performance skills. She is a UW drama graduate and has directed numerous children's stage productions. She is Artistic Director of West Seattle Theatre Arts.

■ **STEVE KUNTZ** **(206) 720-1562**

Musical theatre audition coach for middle and high school drama students. Kuntz is in his eleventh year as music coordinator and artist-in-residence at an arts-oriented private school in Seattle.

4.1 Coaches/Stage

■ **MICHAEL J. LOGGINS**   **(206) 975-3578**

   (See 2.1 Acting Coaches/Stage.)

■ **VALERIE MAMCHES**   **(206) 524-9231**
(Equity, SAG, AFTRA)

   Mamches, who offers private acting and audition coaching, has had more than 25 years' experience as a teacher, actor, director and writer on Broadway and Off Broadway, as well as in regional theatres. She believes in nurturing talent and craft in a safe, supportive manner.

■ **JESSICA MARLOWE-GOLDSTEIN (206) 323-7499**

   (See 2.1 Acting Coaches/Stage.)

■ **GRETCHEN ORSLAND**   **(206) 632-8015**
(Equity, AFTRA)

   Audition coaching for the young actor; Orsland has an MFA in Theatre from Southern Methodist University, and has taught and acted extensively throughout the Seattle area. She is a founding member of Seattle's Bathhouse Theatre, and currently is on the staff at Lakeside School.

ACTING COACHES/ ON-CAMERA

Seattle

■ **LAURA ANNE FERRI**   **(206) 281-9447**
(Equity, SAG, AFTRA)

Commercial and vocal coach (ages 5-18); Ferri is a London-trained (LAMDA) classical actor with extensive film, TV and regional stage experience. She has 15 years of teaching experience, including the Seattle Children's Theatre.

■ **KALLES-LEVINE PRODUCTIONS (206) 447-9318**

Children's Commercial Acting Workshop (ages 5-12). A four-hour class on basic on-camera skills, $65; the third Saturday of each month.

■ **VALERIE MAMCHES**   **(206) 524-9231**

Various classes and workshops in acting for the camera.

■ **ROTHFIELD, RYAN, AND ROTH**   **(206) 448-0927**

One-day intensive acting workshop for on-camera work. Taught by Jodi Rothfield for ages 11-17, $85; and Katie Ryan for ages 6-10, $60.

■ **VERONICA WEIKEL**   **(206) 547-3230**

Commercial voice training for the young actor.

WORKSHOPS
& YOUTH THEATRE

Seattle Area

■ **BAINBRIDGE PERFORMING ARTS**
(206) 842-1163

BPA sponsors evening, weekend and after-school performance workshops for youngsters, teens and adults. Each summer, BPA also offers special three-week sessions in acting and the related disciplines. All workshops (including acting, film, mime, singing and movement) are taught by working professionals.

■ **NORTHWEST ACTORS STUDIO**   **(206) 324-6328**

(See 2.2 Studios.)

■ **SEATTLE CHILDREN'S THEATRE DRAMA**
SCHOOL
P.O. Box 9640
Seattle, WA 98109-0640
(206) 443-0807

SCT is the nation's second-largest resident children's theatre company and drama school. The Drama School offers year-round classes for ages 3½ to 18, including creative drama, beginning through advanced acting and specialty classes including improv and musical theatre. The Young Actor Institute offers a six-week summer intensive in rehearsal techniques, character development, musical theatre and ensemble acting for 14- to 21-year-olds. All sessions are taught by professional theatre artists.

4.3 Workshops & Youth Theatre

■ **SPOTLIGHT YOUTH THEATRE/JCC**
Center Stage
Stroum Jewish Community Center
3801 E Mercer Way
Mercer Island, WA 98040
(206) 232-7115

Contact: Daniel Alpern. Spotlight Youth Theatre is a year-round youth theatre program offering drama education and performance. During the academic year, the program's Spotlight Youth Theatre productions include educational workshops for a nominal tuition fee. Casting is by open audition.

In addition, there is a Black Box Coffee House for teens and a touring company, The Mitzvah Theatre Players, for children ages eight to thirteen. Its Summer Theatre Camp offers either three- or six-week daily drama programs. Instructors are working theatre professionals. (See Center Stage in 1.2 Equity for address.)

■ **STUDIO EAST**
402 - 6th St. S.
Kirkland, WA 98033
(206) 827-3123

Contact: Jennifer Reif, Education Director. Studio East offers year-round classes in theatre, music and dance to students at all levels of ability and experience, including performance-based classes with entrance by audition only. In addition, Studio East offers Little Players, a pre-school program to develop self-esteem through drama. Summer programs include both the six-week Young Actors Professional Intensive for children ages 13 to 20, and two-week summer camps for children ages 8 to 15 in several locations: Kirkland, Ballard, Edmonds, Monroe, Bellevue and Issaquah. All but the pre-school program involve live performances, some for casting directors.

4.3 Workshops & Youth Theatre

■ **VILLAGE THEATRE/KIDSTAGE**
P.O. Box 402
Issaquah, WA 98027
(206) 391-8304

Village Theatre's kidstage program offers year-round classes in theatre arts. The Kidstage Summer Production puts young people in charge of producing a full-length musical. VT's Internship Program offers professional work experience in theatrical production and a stipend to eight individuals per year.

■ **WASHINGTON ACADEMY OF PERFORMING ARTS**
18047 NE 68th St. #B 130
Redmond, WA 98052
(206) 883-2214

Contact: Deborah Hadley. The Academy offers classes in dance, music and theatre for ages three to adult.

■ **WEST SEATTLE THEATRE ARTS**
10015 - 28th SW
Seattle, WA 98146
(206) 935-9782

Contact: Cate Koler. WSTA is a five-year-old company based at the Olympic Heights Hall in West Seattle. It offers instruction in theatre arts during the school year, taught by working professionals. The summer program includes two drama camps and a performing troupe. Two to four productions per year showcase young talent, ages five to 16. Auditions are announced in the newspapers.

4.3 Workshops & Youth Theatre

■ **YOUNG PERFORMERS STUDIO**
114 Alaskan Way S #210
Seattle, WA 98104
(206) 789-2373

Contact: Donnajeanne Goheen. YPS offers small classes in auditioning, on-camera technique, cold reading and improvisation on a regular basis for young performers ages four to 16. Occasionally, classes are offered in voice-over, musical theatre, stage combat and clowning. Fees range from $8 to $12 per hour. Instructors are working actors, directors, and casting professionals.

■ **YOUTH THEATRE NORTHWEST**
P.O. Box 296
Mercer Island, WA 98040
(206) 232-4145

Contact: Sue Clement. YTN is a year-round program of drama education and performances. During the academic year, Youth Theatre Northwest schedules six family-oriented productions, featuring 9- to 18-year-old actors (one of the shows is staged by advanced students). The summer program offers professionally-led drama workshops for children 6 to 20, in five age ranges.

5

In a
Supporting Role

AUDITION TAPES

Seattle & Portland

■ **AUDISEE**
1011 Western Ave. #506
Seattle, WA 98104
(206) 283-4733

Voice demo tapes, $100 per hour to record/mix; $75 hour to edit. Includes direction. Typically works with experienced voice talent who provide their own copy and/or a selection of pre-produced spots.

■ **MACDONALD RECORDING COMPANY**
    (See Pure Audio, below.)

■ **STEVE MITCHELL PRODUCTIONS**
(206) 547-3230

Voice demo tapes, $400; includes all copy, individual direction, music/effects and 25 cassettes. Mitchell and his producer, Veronica Weikel, make sure the talent's agent gets a sample cassette for approval before final copies are made. Talent may also bring in new material to update master tape.

5.1 Audition Tapes

■ **PURE AUDIO RECORDING COMPANY**
2908 First Ave.
Seattle, WA 98121
(206) 728-6300

Voice demo tapes, $250; includes all copy, individual direction, music/effects and five cassettes. A post-taping marketing discussion is also included. (Formerly MacDonald Recording Company.)

■ **REX RECORDING**
1931 SE Morrison
Portland, OR 97214
(503) 238-4525

Voice demo tapes, $60 per hour; includes professional direction (copy available if necessary), music/effects and marketing consultation. Discount prices on cassettes. Cassette dubs are extra.

■ **STUDIO FIVE RECORDING**
13400 Northup Way #2
Bellevue, WA 98005
(206) 643-1755

Voice demo tapes, $210; includes individual direction and production.

Voice Tape Duplication

■ **AMERICAN MOTION PICTURES**	(206) 282-1776
■ **FASTTRAX**	(206)781-0886
■ **BAD ANIMALS/SEATTLE**	(206) 443-1500
■ **PURE AUDIO**	(206) 728-6300
■ **STEVE MITCHELL PRODUCTIONS**	(206) 547-3220

PHOTOGRAPHERS

Seattle

■ **SCOTT AREMAN**   **(206) 728-0686**
   Headshots $110; includes two rolls of 35 mm, 2 proof sheets and one 8x10.

■ **TED D'ARMS**   **(206) 282-2254**
   Headshots, $200 package; includes 3-4 rolls 35mm, 3-6 clothing changes and two 8x10s.

5.2 Photographers

■ **LYNN DEBON** **(206) 292-8717**
Headshots, $80; includes one roll of 35mm and proofs; prints are $15.

■ **MARK LEVIN** **(206) 932-4067**
Headshots, $125; includes one roll of 36 exposures, proofs and two 8x10s. Composites $320; includes four rolls, proofs and six 8x10s.

■ **BEN MARRA** **(206) 624-7344**
Headshots, $150; includes one roll 35mm, proofs and the first 8x10.

■ **GREG NYSTROM** **(206) 286-1452**
Headshots, $95; includes one roll 35mm and one 8x10. Additional prints $15 each.

■ **ANITA RUSSELL** **(206) 746-6506**
Headshots, $75; includes one roll 35mm, proofs, and one 8x10. Composites, $150; includes two rolls, proofs, and two prints.

■ **ROGER SCHREIBER** **(206) 622-3525**
Headshots, $60; includes one unprocessed roll of 35mm.

■ **STEVE STRICKLAND** **(206) 728-1939**
Headshots, $75; one roll 35mm; proofs and one 8X10. (206) 321-5497.

■ **BOB WILLIAMS** **(206) 583-0802**
Headshots $65; includes one roll of 35mm or 120mm and proofs. Prints extra.

H·E·A·D·S·H·O·T·S

ROGER SCHREIBER

PHOTOGRAPHER

6 2 2 · 3 5 2 5

Portland

■ **COLLEEN CAHILL**   **(503) 228-1465**
Headshots, $65 12-18 exposures, one 8 x10 print and contact sheet

■ **OWEN CAREY**   **(503) 249-1772**
Headshots, $155, one roll with one 8x10 print; $210 two rolls with two 8x10s. Appointments in Seattle.

PHOTO LABS

■ **ABC PICTURES**
1867 E Florida
Springfield, MO 65803
(417) 869-9433 or 869-3456

Quantity lithographs of headshots and postcards (500 8x10s, typesetting included, for $80; no backside printing).

■ **MOONPHOTO**
431 Westlake Ave. N
Seattle, WA 98109
(206) 682-7260

Custom quality black/white photo lab; Lake Union district (100 8x10 for $150).

■ **PANDA PHOTOGRAPHIC LAB**
533 Warren Ave. N
Seattle, WA 98109
(206) 285-7091

Custom black/white photo lab; Queen Anne district (100 8x10s for $170 plus copy negative charge).

■ **PRICE PHOTO SERVICES**
6108 Roosevelt Way NE
Seattle, WA 98115
(206) 523-7575

University District photo lab (100 hand-printed 8x10s for $175 plus copy negative charge).

■ **QUANTITY PHOTO**
119 W Hubbard St.
Chicago, IL 60610
(312) 644-8288

Quantity headshot reproductions (100 8x10s: glossy for $47, matte finish for $57, plus copy negative charge).

■ **6TH AVENUE PHOTOGRAPHICS**
1826 Sixth Ave.
Seattle, WA 98101
(206) 682-5060

100 custom (as opposed to machine-printed) 8x10 black and white headshots are $180, plus copy negative charge.

■ **SUPERSHOTS**
971 Goodrich Blvd.
Los Angeles, CA 90022
(213) 724-4809

Specializes in quantity orders of theatrical headshots and composites (100 for $65; each additional 100 for $25).

COSTUMES, MAKE-UP AND HAIR

Costume Resources

■ **COSTUME CREATIONS**
210 W Main
Walla Walla, WA 99362
(509) 525-3703

   Costume manufacturing and design, make-up.

■ **DANCEWEAR NORTHWEST**
5 NE 181st
Portland, OR 97230
(503) 667-6891

   Sequins, rhinestone, fringe, leotards and tights, etc.

■ **JEHLOR FANTASY FABRICS**
730 Andover Park W
Seattle, WA 98188
(206) 575-8250

   Sequined, beaded, metallic fabrics.

Costume Rentals

Seattle

■ **BROCKLIND'S INC.**   (206) 325-8700
500 E Pike (Capitol Hill)

■ **CHAMPION PARTY SUPPLY**   (206) 284-1980
124 Denny Way (Seattle Center)

5.4 Costumes

■ **COSTUMES PERIOD** (206) 735-4235
428 Eighth St. SW #5 (Auburn, WA)

■ **DISPLAY & COSTUME SUPPLY** (206) 362-4810
11201 Roosevelt Way NE (North Seattle)

■ **PACIFIC NORTHWEST COSTUMES**
(206) 881-8618
16129 Redmond Way (Redmond, WA)

Portland

■ **HOLLYWOOD COSTUMERS** (503) 235-9215
635 SE Hawthorne (Portland)

■ **JUDY'S COSTUMES** (503) 620-6488
12705 SW Pacific Hwy. (Tigard, OR)

■ **STAGE WEST** (503) 643-0553
12760 SW First (Beaverton, OR)

■ **VINTAGE VENTURE** (503) 234-0070
6026 NE Glisan (Portland)

5.4 Costumes

Vintage and Resale Clothing Stores

Seattle

■ **DELUXE JUNK**   **(206) 634-2733**
3518 Fremont Pl. N (Fremont)

   Vintage men's and women's clothing, including
formal wear and rhinestone accessories.

■ **FRITZI RITZ**   **(206) 633-0929**
3425 Fremont Pl. N (Fremont)

   1920s to 1960s vintage women's and men's clothing,
formal wear, accessories and costume jewelry.

■ **GUESS WHERE**   **(206) 547-3793**
615 N 35th (Fremont)

   Vintage 1930s to 1950s men's clothing.

■ **ISADORA'S ANTIQUE CLOTHING**   **(206) 441-7711**
1915 1st Ave. (Downtown)

   Vintage men's and women's clothing.

■ **MADAME & CO.**   **(206) 621-1728**
117 Yesler (Pioneer Square)

   Victorian era to the 1940s; Seattle's classiest vintage
woman's shop.

■ **THRIFTKO**   **(206) 789-5357**
85th & First NW (Greenwood)

   Good prices on lots of used contemporary clothing.

■ **VINTAGE CLOTHING**   **(206) 522-5234**
7011 Roosevelt Way NE (Ravenna)

   Best overall selection of authentic 1930s and 1940s
fashions for men and women; great prices, costume rentals
available.

Portland

■ **THE BIG BANG** **(503) 274-1741**
616 SW Park (Portland)

■ **FASHION PASSION** **(503) 223-4373**
616 NW 23rd (Portland)

■ **NAN'S GLAD RAGS** **(503) 642-9207**
21325 SW Tulatin Valley Hwy. (Aloha, OR)

Makeup/Hair/Wigs

■ **SHERRY ANDERS** **(206) 643-3900**
  Hair stylist, makeup artist. (Bellevue, WA)

■ **VICKI GOLDSTEIN-SEZNICK** **(206) 783-9221**
  Makeup artist. (Seattle)

■ **DEIDAMIA MANZABA** **(206) 989-7249**
  Makeup artist. (Seattle)

■ **ILLUSIONARY DESIGNS** **(503) 236-4109**
3558 SE Hawthorne Blvd. (Portland)

■ **PACIFIC NORTHWEST THEATRE ASSOCIATES**
(206) 622-7850

MAKEUP ARTIST
DEIDAMIA MANZABA
989-7249

Index

Loel D. Harvey
Writing Services

Writing, Proofreading,
Copy-Editing,
Substantive Editing

(206) 527-3146